THE
DARK
HILLS

THE DARK HILLS

Rev. Dr. Scott Robinson

SACRED FEET

The Interfaith/Interspiritual/Intra-Tantric
Publishing Imprint of Slate Branch Ashram
The Jones Educational Foundation, Inc. (JEFI)
www.jonesfoundation.net

Published by SACRED FEET
The Interfaith/Interspiritual/Intra-Tantric
Publishing Imprint of Slate Branch Ashram
The Jones Educational Foundation, Inc. (JEFI)
A 501 (c) 3 Not-For-Profit Corporation
P.O. Box 289, Somerset, KY 42502, USA

PHOTO CREDIT
Rev. Dr. Scott Robinson: Allison Ballantine

BOOK & COVER DESIGN
Sandra Simon Mangham

Printed in the United States of America
First published 2015

The SACRED FEET Publishing Imprint
Sw. Shraddhananda, Publisher
Sandra Simon Mangham, Managing Editor

ISBN: 978-0-9915010-3-8

SACRED FEET Publishing Imprint
Mission Statement

The SACRED FEET Publishing Imprint of Slate Branch Ashram is committed to the continuing development and refinement of the discipline of Interfaith Studies and Reflection. As such, SACRED FEET is devoted to bringing high quality Interfaith, Interspiritual, and Intra-Tantric manuscripts into print and appropriate digital formats. Manuscripts must analyze ideas or experiences from two or more religious and/or indigenous spiritual traditions in comparison or intersection with each other and must reflect intellectual as well as spiritual knowledge. SACRED FEET takes as its logo the Guru's *padukas*, or sacred sandals, a symbol indicating that subjects covered in submitted manuscripts must be handled with care and respect. However, manuscripts need not reflect the views of the publisher or editor. Electronic manuscripts with cover letters describing both the project under consideration as well as the author's spiritual journey and intellectual credentials are preferred.

Please contact: Swami Shraddhananda, Saraswati Order of Monastics, Publisher, or Sandra Simon Mangham, Managing Editor, at sacredfeetyoga@gmail.com.

Acknowledgements

My thanks go out to the following people for their help in making this book a reality:

Swami Shraddhananda and Acharya Sandra Chamatkara Mangham at Sacred Feet Publishing for their faith in this project; Jennifer Hanshaw Hackett for her constant and sustaining encouragement and prodigal generosity over several years; Waylon Lewis and Bob Weisenberg at *Elephant Journal*, Joslyn Hamilton at *Recovering Yogi*, and Deshna Ubeda at *Progressive Christianity* for their openness to my thought and promotion of my work, and for permission to rework articles for this book that I originally wrote for their blogs; Andrea Ross for her comments on some of the more difficult chapters; and most of all, my inestimable wife Allison Ballantine, for loving and supporting me long after most people would have given up, I'm sure.

Deep gratitude is due to Audra Czarkinow (1904-1994) for writing "God Walks the Dark Hills," a Southern Gospel classic that inspired the title of this text.

Unless otherwise noted, all quotations from the Psalms are taken from the *Book of Common Prayer* (Church Publishing, 1979.) The sources of other Biblical quotations are identified thus:

NIV (New International Version)
NLT (New Living Translation)
NASB (New American Standard Bible)
ESV (English Standard Version)

Contents

Introduction xiii

III. You Can Observe a Lot by Watching

Introduction

That autobiographer is a fool who believes that his self-revelations will not be regarded as symptoms of psychopathology. —Roy Porter, *A Social History of Madness: The World Through the Eyes of the Insane*

* * *

Siri Tells It Like It Is

I was in a rush to get out the door; I don't remember why, but I was running behind. I bent down to pick up my shoes, and heard the *boop* of Siri being accidentally activated on the cell phone in my front pocket. I swore in savage annoyance. From my pocket, I heard a computer-generated woman's voice say, "I don't talk to you like that, Scott."

If Siri were on all the time, this conversation would probably take place several times a day.

My wife tells me she overheard my younger daughter telling a friend that "My dad gets stressed over little things sometimes." And she's right; I do. Just scratch the surface, and you'll find the anxiety that is the other face of depression just below.

In one of her lectures on the *Course in Miracles*, Marianne Williamson said that mild annoyance is merely a mask for intense fury.[1] I would add that intense fury is simply a substitute for sadness, grief or fear—emotions

---

[1] I heard this gem while driving in a car without a notepad handy, and Williamson's comment made a huge impact on me.

more painful than anger, and with less of an adrenaline payoff. (Depressed teenagers, for instance, have been shown to become "stuck" in angry behavior to the exclusion of sad.) (Kuppens, Allen, Nicholas B. and Sheeber, Lisa, Emotional inertia and psychological maladjustment). But, whatever form the stock of totipotent emotional energy takes, it can be embarrassingly easy to trigger in the form of anger, and trying to choose to feel one's embarrassment, shame, sadness or other, less explosive emotion over acting on anger can be like trying to choose shredded wheat over cupcakes. Anger just feels better.

Up to a point, that is. The impetus for my re-entering therapy after a long hiatus came following a phone conversation I had at our local dog park. I ended up practically screaming into the phone at a UPS dispatcher over an unmade delivery; I won't go into details here, except to say that, even by the hapless dispatcher's admission, I was right. But as she steadfastly refused to deviate from the company policy even to redress my grievance, I became livid out of all proportion to the wrong done to me—something that has happened many times before as I hit the bottom of my recurrent emotional troughs. (Yes, I got the package the next day; even though the dispatcher refused to promise me I would, I'm sure she asked the driver not to make her deal with this crazy man again.) I couldn't return to that dog park for months for sheer embarrassment.

Shortly thereafter, I began work on this book.

If You Live in the Dark a Long Time and the Sun Comes Out

If you live in the dark a long time and the sun comes out, you do not cross into it whistling. There's an initial uprush of relief at first, then—for me, anyway—a profound dislocation. My old assumptions about how the world works are buried, yet my new ones aren't yet operational. There's been a death of sorts, but without a few days in hell, no resurrection is possible. –Mary Karr, *Lit: A Memoir*

* * *

I taught music at an evangelical Christian university for ten years. Though officially adjunct faculty, I worked virtually full time, within one course of a full load and with a studio of private students. When the economy tanked in 2008, it became clear that the fulltime appointment my employers had been dangling before me for years was simply not going to happen—that I was, despite my busy teaching schedule and advanced degrees, going to continue making about half what a convenience store manager makes for as long as I taught there. Every time I hire a sitter so I can come teach, I thought, I am basically paying for the privilege of working here.

So I quit.

Joy and woe, wrote William Blake, are woven fine, and while leaving was indisputably liberating in many ways, the change left me, at the same time, profoundly dislocated—especially during the approach of the first fall semester in ten years for which I had no classes to prepare. But the dark times were always generously laced with a lightness and spaciousness, the fulfillment of being more involved in my children's lives and in their school, and the freedom to discover who I really am and what I really believe, unhampered by the doctrinal statement I signed when I took on my teaching job.

I still missed teaching fiercely, and there was never any question that whatever I ended up doing would be essentially educational. But it took a long time of woolgathering and casting around—which my wife's salary and moral support, happily, enabled me to do—before I began to realize what a person who teaches, preaches, writes, used to lead retreats years ago, has a contemplative nature and composes and performs devotional music should be doing with himself. More and more as I get older, I think I'm going to have to learn to enjoy the journey because I'm never going to "get there."

When the view finally began to clear, I enrolled in the Shalem Institute for Spiritual Formation, a training program for spiritual directors and retreat leaders. I now lead guided labyrinth walks, contemplative workshops and retreats in churches and retreat centers. I also compose and perform interfaith *kirtan*—audience-participatory call-response devotional song rooted in the Hindu tradition, and sometimes known in this country as "yoga chanting." And I work as an on-call hospice chaplain. At the half-century mark, I seem to be getting closer to figuring out what my unusual constellation of gifts has fitted me to do.

Now, you would think that this attainment of relative clarity would make me happy, or at least bring me relief from anxiety. But it's been a long time coming, and it didn't come easy, and there were bleak years to be slogged through in the interval. I found that I had become accustomed to the predictability of my former mired-down life to the point where the prospect of a new, liberated life was daunting. Instead of setting off down the path, I found myself generating all kinds of ways of avoiding it, hiding from change and languishing in the grip of what the Desert Fathers and Mothers called the Noonday Demon—their term for depression and paralyzing languor.

I was for a long time afraid that this new endeavor, like others in the past, would not "work out"—that it would not be, in worldly terms, "successful." What if people don't come to my workshops/attend my kirtans/book me for retreats? The music business has me so gun-shy about relying on other people to validate my work that I sometimes miss the days when I worked on a loading dock. The last thing I want is for ministry to become success-driven.

As a classically trained composer, I had a reasonably good run: a couple major-label recordings, some national broadcasts, a few middling-prestigious grants, and a university teaching job. Not enough to make it to the playoffs, but enough to beat the point-spread, careers in classical composition being what they are.

But as exciting as it is to hear a choir or chamber ensemble perform my music, I have found it a power of magnitude more fulfilling to lead kirtans I have composed myself, with like-minded musicians behind me and a gathering of devoted souls facing me and singing my music back. I had told myself a story—about a contemporary classical composer and academic—for so long, that I had come to believe it without question. The possibility that I may be better fitted for another life was completely obscured by the life I had constructed for myself. Only when I had learned that my self-made life was a sham was I able to let go of it, leaving me free to accept the real life for which I was made, and to which I was being called by God.

"For whoever wants to save their life will lose it, but whoever loses their life for me will save it." (Luke 9:24)

Interfaith Ministry

"Interfaith minister? What's that?"

I am a Christian, meaning that I find God in and through Jesus of Nazareth. In the parlance of interfaith ministry, Christianity is my "home tradition." Specifically, I belong to the Episcopal Church, and I am a professed member of the Third Order of St. Francis, a non-conventual Episcopalian religious order.

But by ordination, I am an interfaith minister, trained at The New Seminary for Interfaith Studies and ordained by the Interfaith Temple in New York City. To Christians who believe that followers of Jesus must make exclusive truth claims for our own tradition, and to others who think all Christians make those claims, this may seem a contradiction. But not all Christians believe that non-Christians are, by definition, "unsaved." I often say, in the language of some forms of Hinduism,[2] that Jesus is my *ishta devata*, or "chosen ideal." My choice is not meant to imply that other choices are invalid. As the motto of the New Seminary, given to it by founder and interfaith pioneer Rabbi Joseph Gelberman, says, "Never instead-of; always in-addition-to."

If I had to name a philosophical school behind my interfaith orientation, it would be *perennialism*—a school of

---

[2] "Hinduism" is a problematic term, invented by the British and lumping together a great many religious traditions of the Indian sub-continent. Nevertheless, as this book is not a treatise on the differences between Gaudiya Vaishnavism and Kashmir Shaivism or the like, I use it throughout for the sake of convenience.

thought that posits a thread of truth and wisdom running through all faith traditions, manifesting itself in each in ways that are specific to that tradition, yet always recognizable to those who are attentive to them. While all faiths are certainly not the same, and the differences between them are important, perennialism says there are identifiable themes, tropes and patterns they all share to one degree or another.

Modern perennialism, which had antecedents as far back as the sixteenth century, was founded by Indologist, art historian and religious thinker Ananda Coomaraswamy, in collaboration with René Guénon and Frithjof Schuon, two Western converts to Sufi Islam. T.S. Eliot, Thomas Merton and Huston Smith are among the best-known modern perennialists. (Caldecott) You will see a rather crude form of perennialism at work in the way I careen from one religious tradition to another in quest of images and metaphors to convey my own thought. Perennialism "is in fact an exceptionally powerful and flexible tool for the interpretation of religious forms—philosophies, theologies, mythology and symbolism in general." (Caldecott 618)

So what is interfaith ministry? My elevator-speech answer is this: *As an Interfaith Minister, I am prepared to minister to people of any faith or no faith, in whatever way their needs require and consciences permit.* In hospital and hospice settings, that means I have prayed Hebrew prayers with Jewish patients and their families, chanted the Hare Krishna Maha Mantra with Hindus, "prayed like a Muslim" (according to a kind Muslim patient) anointed the sick, administered emergency infant baptisms, and imposed ashes on Protestant and Catholic alike on Good Friday. Outside that setting, I draw upon Judeo-Christian, Hindu, Buddhist and Sufi traditions (and others on occasion as required) in my various ministry activities. Likewise, I have, throughout this book, used the language and thought, not only of my own tradition, but also of other traditions (notably Hinduism and Buddhism) that particularly interest me.

During my ten years at an evangelical Christian university, I was expected to adhere to the doctrinal statement I had signed as a condition of employment. As time went on and my worldview developed, it took an ever-increasing amount of mental gymnastics to keep myself believing I believed what I was supposed to believe. When I left that job, the dam burst.

At my wife's suggestion, I began writing a blog, one of the first entries in which I documented the rapid shift in my personal belief system. The growing conviction, present with me since childhood, that there are many paths up one mountain, would no longer be denied. So that there may, from the outset, be no misunderstandings about the faith framework of this book, I include an edited version of that entry here:

Bare Earth, Clean Paper[ii]

Does anyone write something where something has been already written?
Or plant a sapling where one already grows?
No: he looks for a blank piece of paper,
and sows the seed where none has yet been sown.
Brother, sister: be bare earth,
be clean paper, untouched by writing,
so that you may be ennobled by the pen of revelation—
so that the Gracious One may sow seed within you. —Jalaluddin Rumi, tr. Camille Helminski

"Freedom, O Freedom!" is the cry of the soul. —Vivekananda, "What is Religion?"

* * *

Dear God:

I have learned something in these past weeks. I have been more radically taken apart and put back together since classes ended last spring than at any other period. Yet, looking back, I can see clearly that these changes have been a long time coming—that I have been holding them back, in fact. There has been a slow buildup of pressure over so long a time as to render it unnoticeable, followed by a violent acceleration and release precipitated by an event whose consequences were unforeseen. So now, something I have long toyed with wanting, played at wanting, considered the possibility of wanting some day: I actually want it now—intensely want it.

I want to die.

Unless a grain of wheat falls into the ground and dies, it remains a grain, and nothing more—but if it dies, it bears much fruit. (John 12:24)

God, help me to bear fruit; help me to die.

I am so heartily weary of myself. My every breath shouts, "I, I, I, I, I." Let me disappear to myself; give me rest from the unremitting labor of self-assertion. Let me be a witness, an observer, a passerby.[3]

All my life, I have asked You to help me, but what I have actually meant is, Do it for me. I have asked You for strength, but what I have wanted is ease. I would have every valley raised, every mountain made low—but without my having to die first. I do not ask You for this any longer. I ask to die.

I do not ask You to help me find the way You have set before me. I do not even know for sure that You have set one, and if You have, I understand now that I must find it myself. Help me to look, to listen. Help me to quiet the roaring in my head that shouts down Your still, small voice. I have barricaded myself against You, and I do not ask You to storm the barricades; I ask only that I may persevere in dismantling them myself.

My world is a sealed room, arranged just the way I like it.[4] Only it isn't: the windows leak, the door doesn't latch, and I am forever fighting to keep my room the way I want it. Help me open up my room to the whole noisy, untidy world; I am weary of defending it.

My universe has been so narrow, and I have tried to confine You within its compass. (Forgive me; I did it in love.) You set the seas their boundaries which they may not cross, but Your children You have created for freedom. *You have not received the spirit of slaves that leads you into fear again. Rather, you have received the spirit of God's adopted children by which we call out,*

---

[3] See Gospel of Thomas, Saying 42
[4] I have borrowed this metaphor from Pema Chödrön.

"Abba! Father!" (Romans 8:15)

Now, if any would say, "You must use these songs, these sacraments," I will not listen; and if any would set themselves up between me and You, I will not heed them; and if any would deny the freedom of my soul, they shall be to me as a venomous serpent: a beloved creation of Yours, to be avoided for my own safety.

And surely Vivekananda discerned You;
And surely Lawrence of the Resurrection labored with You;
And surely Teresa built a castle for You;
And surely Black Elk saw visions from You;
And surely Rumi sang of You;
And surely Francis gave all for You;
And surely Socrates questioned after You;
And surely Bach musicked Your creation;
And surely Elisha put on You like a garment;
And surely the Buddha served You in noble silence;
And surely in Jesus You lived our life and died our death;
And surely in Him, I will rise as He did.

And if any would chant *Om* to the Resplendent Lord, I
    would be a *bhakta* among them;
And if any would ponder the Impersonal Absolute, I would
    sit down, a *yogi* among them;
And if any would shout salvation's story in concert with the
    blood-washed band, I would lift up my voice with
    theirs;
And if any would sing *la illaha il Allah* in the whirling dance,
    I would polish the mirror of my heart with them;
And if any would commune with angels and archangels and

all the company of heaven, I would receive Your Body and Blood with them.

Jesus, as my vision grows greater, You do not diminish within it—rather, You grow greater, too. My devotion to You increases as the universe around You expands, as the radiance of a jewel is increased by its setting.

Let me never try to force You back into that narrow space; let me never begin a sentence with "God couldn't;" let me be bare earth, clean paper.

My little girl wants to walk along the top of a wall. "Hold my hand, Daddy," she says. She is eager to walk, but unsteady and fearful. Steady my footsteps; bolster my willing but timorous spirit. At the right time, take away Your hand.

I am learning.

The Poisoned Arrow

The Buddha told a story of a young warrior who, being felled by a poisoned arrow, would not allow it to be removed until he knew who had shot him, from what tribe the archer came, and of what kind of wood the shaft was made. Likewise, there is a point of diminishing returns on running to ground the reasons for our suffering, and if that detective work prevents us from doing what is needful for ameliorating that suffering, it is not serving us. Neither is there much to be gained, I think, from confessing other peoples' sins.

In that spirit, I am not going to dwell more than is necessary in these pages on what I think "caused" my own experiences of depression. Throughout, I will advert, as needed, to various items in my personal backpack of suffering, but I will try not to waste too much of your time with my own origin myth.

"I shall never learn what 'caused' my depression," wrote novelist William Styron, "as no one will ever learn about their own. To be able to do so will likely forever prove to be an impossibility, so complex are the intermingled factors of abnormal chemistry, behavior and genetics." (Styron)

Most of the positive comments I got on my blog entries—particularly those in which I wrote about my depression—were about how much people were helped by things in my writing that resonated with their own experience, making them feel less alone, more understood. This book will succeed to the extent that it does that for you.

Book Overview

This book is not "about" depression in the sense that it treats of nothing else. Some of the thoughts herein are about depression, certainly—but others are rather the thoughts of a person living with depression, about a variety of more or less germane topics. You will not, however, encounter the thoughts of a severely depressed person, because during those times I could not write. It's probably just as well.

The book is divided into three parts:

Part One, *The Foul Rag and Bone Shop of the Heart* (named for a line in W.B. Yeats's poem, "The Circus Animals' Desertion",) is part memoir and part meditation, examining depression through the lenses of Scripture, events in the news, and my own experience.

Part Two, *The Road to Real,* sets forth my own ideas about the sources and meaning of suffering—that is, what makes us suffer, and for what reasons, if any, and what we might do to redeem the experience of suffering.

Part Three, *You Can Observe a Lot by Watching* (apologies to Yogi Berra), is about spiritual practice—both in theory and in a hands-on, what-works-for-me way.

Wisdom and Stuff

I…found that the research I had been doing for this book, whether it was to be of value to anyone else or not, was terrifically useful to me.
–Andrew Solomon, *The Noonday Demon: An Atlas of Depression*

* * *

Although the last section of this book does include some spiritual practices that have worked for me, there is very little in the way of advice in this book. There is, however, a certain amount of what a few kindly-disposed people have been generous enough to call "wisdom." Don't be fooled.

One of the best things about any kind of creative endeavor is that it puts us in touch with bits of our brains to which we do not ordinarily have access. I'm sure that everyone who makes art has regarded a new novel, painting, poem, play, film, sculpture, symphony or song and thought, "I didn't know I knew all that." What we make teaches us, and I am at least as much in need of everything in this book as you are—probably more. If we ever meet and you are expecting me to actually live by all this so-called wisdom, you will be disappointed. As my friend, the Sufi singer-songwriter Naila Schulte, sings, "I'm singing to you, but I'm talking to me."

My Approach to Scripture

You may find my approach to Scripture unusual. I do not find in Scripture primarily morality, nor, certainly, literal history as the Fundamentalists do. My approach is primarily mythic; my exegesis is to look for points of contact between Scripture and life as I live it and see it lived. I generally look first for connections to my own experience.

For instance: before we left on our honeymoon in Greece, a friend who is a classics scholar gave us this heads-up: *The gods of Olympus are very much alive.* I little understood what he meant until we were ensconced in the highlands of Epirus, near the Albanian border. We were staying in a little village called Tsepelovo, where the owner of the guesthouse introduced us to an English expatriate couple who had just opened a tourist lodge in the tiny nearby village of Kikouli. The couple took us under their wing and showed us around their village one evening—separately, to avoid scandalizing any of the kerchiefed matrons with the company of an unknown man.

As I relaxed in the home of Petros, the village postman, in a living room with Ottoman-style divans, or raised cushioned platforms, lining all the walls in place of furniture, my host reclining on an elbow while his wife brought me a tasty dish of broad beans and spinach, I realized what my friend had meant: Zeus Xenios, the God of Travelers, still animated these people who had been among the first to embrace the Gospel some two thousand years ago. The "guest-friendship" of Homeric epic is still, for them, one of "the deep themes that tell the myths we live." (Moore) (I found the same spirit in Turkey; *buyunuz*, or "help yourself," was one of the first words I learned there.) The myths of Zeus and of Hestia, Goddess of the Hearth, are still a motive force in people's daily lives.

What is the source of a myth's power? Not its historicity, certainly; some myths are based in historical events, while others are pure invention. Nor is it the aesthetic power of the narrative itself; many myths are downright bizarre—even grotesque and disturbing—and while there are legions of beautiful stories, very few of them aspire to the mythic.

I think the power of a myth lies in the contact it makes with our selves, psychologically and spiritually. Myths are universal and eternal, but also deeply personal and subjective—and that subjectivity, the fact that one can actually experience the dynamics of myth in one's own life, is what makes myths true and powerful. If you have not lived through something, the poet Kabir tells us, it is not true. (Kabir) Myths become true to the extent that they become true *for us*.

A true hero, wrote Garrison Keillor, has the power to give us the gift of a larger life. (Keillor, "The Babe") When we allow myths to be present in our daily struggles and sufferings, those struggles and sufferings become ennobled, "connected to the stars, a part of the mind of God." Our little daily deaths become the stuff of new and larger life.

"You're gonna have a baby, Rosasharn," Ma Joad told her pregnant daughter in John Steinbeck's *The Grapes of Wrath*, "and that's somepin to you lonely and away. That's gonna hurt you, an' the hurt'll be a lonely hurt, an' this here tent is alone in the worl', Rosasharn...They's a time of change, an' when that comes, dyin' is a piece of all dyin', and bearin' is a piece of all bearin', an bearin' an' dyin' is two pieces of the same thing. An' then things ain't lonely any more. An' then a hurt don't hurt so bad, cause it ain't a lonely hurt no more, Rosasharn. I wisht I could tell you so you'd know, but I can't." (Steinbeck 209)

This is when we become illuminated by the mythic—when, for us, birthing becomes a piece of all birthing, dying a piece of all dying. All pain, all comfort, all people.

This is why I like the way Buddhist teacher Pema Chödrön describes the difficultioo of life as "juicy." It reminds me of my undergraduate organ teacher's explanation of why to hold on to a discord a little longer than its strict rhythmic value indicates: "You want to *squeeze* a dissonance," he told me, "because that's where the *juice* is." Instead of fleeing from difficulty and discomfort, we can lean into them, squeeze them, because the really nourishing stuff is not to be found in what goes smoothly, but in what grates.

The trouble is that while our lives are plenty grating and painful and juicy, our myths have lost all their nubbliness through un- or over-familiarity, so that we fail to see the stories we are living. Like most of Scripture, the very roughness that made the old stories stick has been smoothed away to the point where they now seem simply outlandish tales—like the Greek myths—or the rarefied stuff of stained-glass windows, whose hagiographies and Bible stories seem to have no relevance to our actual experience. "The old words of grace," wrote novelist Walker Percy, "are worn smooth as poker chips and a certain devaluation has occurred, like a poker chip after it has been cashed in." (Percy) Our myths are all around us, and we never claim them for our own because we do not recognize them and they have lost their sticking power for us.

Of course, sometimes myths do stick—and burn, like slow napalm. I have long been sympathetic to Cain, for instance, in the Genesis myth. Cain worked hard and gave his best, but God rejected Cain's offering of produce while accepting Abel's animal sacrifice. How is that fair? Why did God accept Abel's offering of a dead animal and reject Cain's offering of first fruits? Some scholars believe the prototype of this story goes back to a time of conflict between ancient Sumerian pastoralists and agriculturalists. So is everyone meant to be a herdsman, and no one a farmer? Commentaries on Genesis 4 do a lot of speculating about Cain, supposing that his heart was not in the right place when he made his offering—or they drag in Hebrews and 1 Peter and say that without blood there is no forgiveness of sin. But both of these interpretations are examples of *eisegesis*—reading ideas into the text rather than out of it. The fact is that the chapters preceding Cain and Abel's offerings don't say anything at all about blood sacrifice or Cain's state of mind. All it says in the text is that God "had regard" for Abel's offering, and for Cain's offering God had "no regard." Most of us know what came next: Cain killed Abel in a jealous rage.

Every time I see some people succeed because they know how to work the system, while others—no less able or hardworking fail because they don't know how to ingratiate themselves with the gatekeepers of success, I think of Cain and Abel. "The children of this world," Jesus said, "are more shrewd in dealing with the world around them than are the children of the light." (Luke 16:8b) And while Cain may or may not have been more enlightened than Abel, maybe he killed Abel less because he was evil than because he found he'd been rooked.

Jesus also told a story about a brother who got the shaft. One of the Jesuits at the college I went to told me that he hated the parable of the Prodigal Son (Luke 15:11-31.) He said he always felt sorry for the dutiful older brother, who stayed home, worked hard and behaved responsibly—and never squandered the family fortune on prostitutes as his younger brother did.

Look! All these years I've been slaving for you and never disobeyed your orders. Yet you never gave me even a young goat so I could celebrate with my friends. But when this son of yours who has squandered your property with prostitutes comes home, you kill the fattened calf for him! (NIV)

Traditionally pious interpretation of this story says that we are all in the position of the irresponsible younger brother relative to God, and that to identify with the dependable elder brother is a sign of self-righteousness—but I don't think one needs to be particularly sanctimonious to think that the elder brother got the short end of the stick.

Everyone lives a theology, one of my students[5] once said, whether he or she articulates one or not. The life we live proclaims the God in whom we believe, so it is good to

---

[5] Jonathan Wilson-Hartgrove

pay attention to what we say with our lives. Likewise, we can gain a lot by becoming aware of the myths we live.

Sometimes myths work covertly beneath the surface, like the Oedipus and Elektra myths during our sexual maturation (if we are to believe Freud.) But if we become aware of them, and of how they intersect with our own reality, we can open ourselves up to them so that they become a source of power, entering into our quotidian lives and lighting them up from the inside, like a candle in a Chinese lantern. They can make us see the resonance and gravitas of our lives as lived.

The Easter myth should do that for me; the death and resurrection of Jesus is, after all, the main event of the Christian faith. It's really what we hang our hats on. "If Christ has not been raised," Paul told the church at Corinth, "your faith is futile." (1 Corinthians 15:17)

Many of my happiest childhood memories are of Easter—the music, the flowers, the return of spring after the long Upstate New York winter, the general good mood of everyone around me and the wonderful story at the center of everything. When I was a kid, the giddy triumphalism of Easter was enough—and Easter still "works" on me: still fills me with profound gratitude and a warm sense of well-being. But as I grow older, I find that that is no longer enough. I want to live Easter—want it to light me up from inside. If you have not lived through something, it is not true.

"No one takes (my life) from me," Jesus told his disciples, "but I lay it down of my own accord. I have authority to lay it down and authority to take it up again." (John 10:18) But do I have a life worth laying down? Is there any meaning in sacrificing what I never really made anything of by worldly standards?

I built a life for myself—the life of a composer-academic. I can't say from this distance why I built that Frankenstein's monster of a life, but I did, and it took an enormous outlay of time, effort and cash to do it. Maybe that would be a worthy sacrifice. But that life never amounted to much, as it turned out, and it didn't really seem to be going anywhere when I walked away from it in 2008. There's a Hindu story about a farmer pouring threshed grain out of a tower so the wind could carry away the chaff; when the wind unexpectedly picked up and began blowing away the grain, too, he decided to give that grain to God, since it wasn't going to do him any good anyway. Obviously, there is no merit in a "sacrifice" like that.

Besides, something in me still clings to that life. Though I have turned my back on it, I have never really let it die. I still hear things on NPR and think, "I should download a podcast of that for my class"—still read things in the paper and mark how useful they would be as teaching aids. I still fantasize about the university seeing the error of its ways and calling to ask me to accept a fulltime job, with time already served counting toward tenure. Even though part of me believes that "clinging to life causes life to decay," while "the life that is freely given is eternal"[6]—even though I dearly want to lay down that life and be raised to a new one—I have not yet pulled the plug on my do-it-yourself life.

Maybe the paste-up life I made for myself—father, husband, performer, musician, writer, teacher—is what I need to be prepared to let go of, so that the essential kernel of me can bear fruit. Maybe we all need to be prepared to give up everything that we think makes us identifiable—all

---

[6] Principles of the Third Order of St. Francis

those passing-away autobiographical things we have so laboriously put on like stage costumes. If that's what needs to die in order for the radiant new creation to be born—if that's what it will take for the Easter myth to shine in me from within—then God help me to give it. Let me lay it all down, trusting in the gift of a larger life, so that if any come seeking the old, false me in days to come, Easter may shine through me, saying, *Why do you look for the living among the dead? He is not here; he is risen!*

Gods and Goddesses and Devas, Oh My![iii]

You shall have no other gods before Me. –Exodus 20:3

There may be readers, especially Christian ones, who will struggle with my references to Hinduism throughout this book. Whilst many Christians can feel more or less at home around Judaism, and a few even around Islam, polytheistic religions like Hinduism often give them the heebie-jeebies. I had similar struggles myself.

There are different ways of understanding the panoply of Hindu gods and goddesses. Millions believe that each divinity has an independent, objective existence, that their physical appearance is as depicted in Indian devotional art, and that everything the *Puranas* say about the gods is literally true.

Swami Vivekananda, in his book *Jnana Yoga*, maintains that the gods have a real existence, but that they are roles rather than persons—positions filled by a succession of human souls who are not yet ready for full liberation and who exercise divine functions until they burn through their good karma and are reborn to give it one more shot.

Shankara, the father figure of Advaita (Non Dualist) Vedanta, said that the gods have a "provisional" existence, to be left behind when the devotee attains to knowledge of the Absolute, which is beyond all concepts and attributes. Ramanuja and the other Bhakti-Vedanta teachers, on the other hand, insisted that the personal God was not a stop-gap and was never to be dispensed with. (Christian theology enthusiasts may discern parallels between the Shankara/Ramanuja dispute and the Paul Tillich/Karl Barth dispute. Very simply put, Tillich sought the transcendent God "behind" the Scriptures, while Barth insisted that God is fully revealed in the Scriptures, and there is nothing beyond them.) "For them the Supreme Being is Person with attributes and there is no Absolute beyond Him." (Tapasyananda)

In Tantric thought, the whole universe is a vast field of energy, all of it in constant vibration, and all of the phenomenal world is merely the cosmic energy vibrating at different frequencies. (You may notice that this theory bears a resemblance to some aspects of modern physics. As a friend of mine who worked at an "occult" bookstore used to say, "the ancients stole all our best ideas.") The same goes for the noumenal world: the gods, or "deity vibrations", as one hears Tantrics say, are the cosmic energy vibrating at divine frequencies. (The "spiritual science" of mantra is based on this idea, the belief being that the Sanskrit names of the deities are the deities themselves in the form of sound vibration.)

One modern approach is to regard the various deities as projections; I heard Bhagavan Das say that "all the gods and goddesses of India are externalizations of the internal process"—an approach similar to the one Jung took toward the Greek pantheon. My own position lies somewhere between that and the classic monotheistic understanding that God, while a unity, is beyond human conceptualization, and that the myriad deities all represent different aspects of the Universal Absolute. In Hindu terms, *Ishvara*, the Personal God in all his and her forms, has a merely provisional existence, whereas *Brahman* is the Universal Absolute, pure Being beyond name, form and qualities, and the various provisional "gods" are merely faces and forms through which we can approach the Absolute.

The "false gods" of the Hebrew Bible were local and tribal divinities, whose devotees were caught up in an ongoing game of "my deity can kick your deity's ass." At the time that the Torah was written, no other near-eastern people but the Jews could even conceive of a single, universal god. So the way I see it, the "gods of the nations" were false because of their limitedness and particularity, not because they spoke other languages than Hebrew and went by other names than "I AM."

The Hindu deities, on the other hand, have long been understood by philosophers to represent various manifestations of the one God who is beyond all human conceptions. In the temple complex at Dakshineswar, Sri Ramakrishna used to tell people that "in this temple, God is worshipped as Kali; in that temple, God is worshipped as Shiva; in that temple, as Radhakanta." (M) When you stand at the south pole, every direction is north.

(If you want to see the real "idols" of American life, look no further than reality TV—a showcase of the hunger for fame, greed for money and wanton sexual indulgence— "the lust of the flesh, the lust of the eyes and the boastful pride of life", (1 John 2:16) in Biblical terms—that stand between human beings and God more effectively than any golden calf ever could.)

Moreover, the various names of the deities have literal meanings that can serve as descriptors as well as proper names. For instance, I found a listing of "108 Names of the Lord Jesus Christ in Sanskrit," and was startled to see that one of them was "Mahavishnu"—"Great Vishnu," one of the so-called "Hindu trinity" of Shiva, Brahma and Vishnu. When I learned that "Vishnu" literally means "all-seeing," it made sense.

Similarly, I love to chant *Om namo Bhagavate Vasudevaya* because, in addition to being one of the names of Krishna, "Vasudeva" also means "shining one who dwells in all beings"—which reminds me of the baptismal vow in the *Book of Common Prayer*, to "seek and serve Christ in all persons, loving your neighbor as yourself."

It is for these reasons that I am able to chant mantras addressed to Shiva and Kali without feeling that I am betraying the Judeo-Christian conception of God with which I was reared. But the question that plagued me was: what does it mean to invoke a deity with no independent personal existence?

For a long time, my Christian scruples prompted me to compose music only for chant texts addressed to *nirguna Brahman*—the impersonal, non-specific Ground of Being: literally, "God without personal attributes." *Sachidananda*, or "Being-Knowledge-Bliss," is one such *nirguna* designation. Only when I began to see the various deities as different aspects of God, as "father," "husband," "teacher," "writer" and "musician" are different aspects of myself, did I feel freed to chant to Krishna, Durga and Ganesha—that is, to *saguna Brahman*, or "God with personal attributes." After all, you cannot even see all of a human being at once, let alone all of God.

[i] "If You Live in the Dark a Long Time and the Sun Comes Out" first appeared in *Elephant Journal* on September 1, 2011, in slightly different form. Used here by permission.

[ii] "Bare Earth, Clean Paper" first appeared in *Elephant Journal* under the title, "Who Does This Christian Guy Think He Is, Anyway?" on August 23, 2010, in slightly different form. Used here by permission.

[iii] A version of this section first appeared under the title "A Christian Yogi Comes to Grips with the Hindu Deities" in *Elephant Journal* on February 2, 2012. Used here by permission.

PART I

The Foul Rag and Bone Shop
of the Heart

Our mental business is carried on much in the same way as the business of the state: a great deal of hard work is done by agents who are not acknowledged. —George Eliot, *Adam Bede*

-Chapter One-

The Noonday Demon[iv]

I moved as through a fog. My senses were dulled and my perception impaired. One day, I sent a check to our health insurance carrier for the entire checking account balance, instead of the payment due. I forgot important meetings. I lost keys, gloves, and once, even my car in a parking lot. —Amy Weintraub, *Yoga for Depression*

All that we are is the result of what we have thought. —The Buddha, *Dhammapada*

* * *

I realize now that I struggled with depression for a long time before I knew I had it. Like Hamlet, I simply found weary, stale, flat and unprofitable all the uses of this world, and it took a long time to figure out that the problem wasn't with the world, but with me.

I suspect I was living with incipient depression even as a child; one of my summer camp counselors described me as "melancholy" while I was in middle school. Growing up, I consciously identified with Charlie Brown, the failure-faced loser from Charles Schultz's *Peanuts* cartoons. As I grew older, the melancholy shape-shifted into anger, desperation to "succeed", and other dysfunctional and self-destructive emotional and behavioral patterns. But I understand now that however much I attempted to distract myself from it, it never really went away.

But the melancholy blossomed into unignorable depression after the birth of my first daughter. This may seem strange, especially since I was (and still am) crazy about my children. But for some reason, depression "can also be caused by positive change. Having a baby, getting a promotion, or getting married are almost as likely to kindle depression as a death or loss." (Solomon 47)

While Clare was still a baby and before Sophie was born, I began wasting time. Lots of time. I spent hours and hours playing computer solitaire. When I became aware of YouTube, things went downhill very fast. Although I have never owned a television, and prided myself on never having seen Friends or Seinfeld or Survivor, I have watched thousand upon thousands of videos on YouTube.

Looking back, I remember being addicted to television as a child, which, I realize, is the real reason I have never owned one as an adult. As an unhappy kid— bullied, belittled, and socially isolated—I gave many, many hours to the worship of the vacuum-tubed god, and like any god worthy of the name, it gave me what I prayed for: "the pervasive sense, in watching it, that life is somewhere other than where you are." (Monbiot)

This sense that life-as-lived is not "real" life stole many productive years from me. While I generally worked hard at whatever I was doing, I constantly felt like my day-to-day existence was a mere preliminary to the "real" life that was surely coming. As my fortieth birthday approached, I finally began to wonder if my "real" life was the one I was already living.

In one sense, becoming a father was the wake-up call I needed; nothing sorts out your sense of what's real and urgent like a dirty diaper. Having tiny, helpless beings utterly dependent on me set off the This Is Not A Drill alarm I had been waiting for.

But as the romance of early fatherhood faded into

an afterglow, the old sense that this cannot really be what life actually is reasserted itself with a vengeance, manifesting itself in inattention to my duties and surroundings, and preoccupation with imagined futures and pasts.

A year before leaving my university teaching job, I became obsessed with a country song about a musician hitchhiking from New England to his home in Raleigh, North Carolina. I played a recording of it in the car over and over and sang it whenever I wasn't playing it. Something in the song was able to bring healing balm within a few inches of the wound that had been growing on my heart for years. The fumes didn't heal me, but they made healing seem tantalizingly close.

The song confronted me with a lost version of myself: the me that would thumb a ride when necessary, and picked up hitchhikers and listened to their stories—that would bicycle thirty miles to a friend's graduation party and crash on her couch—that backpacked around Britain and could make a meal of a cup of soup and two slices of bread for 35p in the youth hostel, or take up with some young actors I'd met at a festival and spend the night on their marble floor—that slept in the loft of an outdoor theater and washed in icy well-water from a pump. A person capable of spontaneity and able to dispense with creature comforts. A romanticized self, surely, but with (I believe) a reality beyond that of mere memoir—and a far, far cry from the constrained, circumscribed person I had become. The feelings the song gave me threw into relief the problem Garrison Keillor identified: "how to be more the good person we set out to be when we were nineteen instead of this dull greedy old weasel snarfing all the food on the plate who we turned into instead." (Keillor, "Al Denny," 261) If I had never been that other person, then why would I miss that person so terribly?

More than anything else, I wanted to be free. The constant round of preparing lectures, grading papers, changing diapers, cooking meals, addictive behaviors, never going anywhere out of an unwillingness to saddle any teenaged babysitter with an infant and a toddler, waiting for a promotion that never came, and trying to get someone, *anyone*, to perform the culturally irrelevant music I was trained to write made me feel trapped, and something from the murky depths of me reached up and snatched at hopes, plans, ambitions—even songs—and clutched them fiercely, hoping they would lead me to freedom and peace. Through that song, I was trying to tell me something. Soon after, I announced my intention to quit my teaching job.

While leaving my job relieved me of the increasingly unrewarding tasks associated with it, it also removed structure from my life upon which, I was to learn, I had become far more dependent than I realized. I went from being constantly harried to being often at loose ends, and my anxiety, irritability and sadness intensified.

As my condition worsened, I became increasingly scatterbrained. Our aging retriever needs to go outside more often, and more urgently, than our younger dog, and during the depth of my first depressive episode, I let him out and forgot about him so often that one of our neighbors began threatening to call the Humane Association. I once tried to pay my children's Quaker school tuition out of my band checking account, which couldn't half cover it. I forgot meetings and appointments (including two with my bishop.) It was as though I had gone from dragging anchor to being rudderless and adrift.

Loss—"of a valued person, or a role, or an idea about yourself" (Solomon 48)—is one of the most common triggers for depression. In my case, the loss of my role—in fact, of my self-constructed identity—as a composer-academic threw my chronic low-grade depression into hyperdrive.

I was self-employed for many years before I began teaching, cobbling together a livelihood out of composing, performing and temp work. I was always self-disciplined; during grad school, I regularly rose at 5:00 a.m. to write music. But after leaving my teaching job, I became unable either to face my obligations, or to take pleasure in constructive diversions. It was as though my mind were in open rebellion against the things I was asking it to do.

Screwtape, the senior demon invented by C.S. Lewis in his book, *The Screwtape Letters*, wrote to his nephew Wormwood, a novice tempter out on his first assignment, about people like me:

> *As the uneasiness and his reluctance to face it cut him off more and more from all real happiness...you will find that anything or nothing is sufficient to attract his wandering attention...You can make him do nothing at all for long periods...All the healthy and outgoing activities which we want him to avoid can be inhibited and nothing given in return, so that at last he may say, as one of my own patients said on his arrival down here, "I now see that I spent most of my life in doing neither what I ought nor what I liked".*
> (Lewis 42)

Ultimately, between the fatigue brought on by staying up late every night surfing the internet—on top of the fatigues of having infant and a toddler in the house—my corrosive shame and the weariness of hiding it, I became irascible and intolerant with my family, lashing out in self-righteous impatience at the least provocation. By the grace of God I woke up enough to see what I was doing to my loved ones, and realized that I needed help.

(It wasn't until years later—when I began doing research for this book—that I learned that keeping late hours is a common behavior for the depressed, both because a depressed person's capacity for getting anything done is greatest at night, and because one's chances of falling asleep are greater if one stays up to the point of utter fatigue. (Strauss 143) Both of these reasons certainly applied to me, though I didn't know for a long time that they were "normal.")

I found a therapist and got a prescription for a mild antidepressant, which took the edge off enough for me to think a little more clearly. But I discovered that while drugs can help manage negative feelings, they can do nothing about negative habits. "Antidepressants help those who help themselves." (Solomon 88) For years, with the apathy and despair gone, when I no longer wanted to sleep all day and was no longer smothering under the weight of a leaden sky full of black clouds, I still struggled with what the Desert Fathers called "afflictive thoughts." I could be out with my children, taking them someplace we all like to be on a beautiful day, and the thought "I'm so unhappy" would come out of nowhere. Or "I'm so miserable!" Literally, those words. And the strange thing is that the words *weren't true;* at that point, I really wasn't miserable. But I was in the habit of telling myself that I was. And to this day these thoughts—and doubtless many, many others, unlanguaged and unrecognized—slide unbidden down tracks I laid for them long ago. And it takes colossal effort to pull up those tracks, and constant vigilance over what I am thinking, so that I now understand the challenge in

Paul's advice to "take every thought captive for Christ." (2 Corinthians 10:5) Swami Vivekananda said that most of us are like spoilt children, and we let our minds think whatever they want to. Not letting the mind default into old destructive patterns is a huge undertaking which, though made more doable though the relief offered by chemical intervention, cannot be accomplished except by laborious effort.

The yogis call these patterns *samskaras*, or "volitional formations." The idea behind *karma* is that everything we think, do or will leaves "traces" in the *vritti*, or mind-stuff, which will pre-dispose us to continue to think, act and will in those ways. "Our deeds determine us," wrote George Eliot, "as much as we determine our deeds." (Eliot) Once samskaras—literally, "what has been put together"—have been established, they must work themselves out completely. (Psychology and neuroscience recognize these patterns, too, the former calling them "conditioned habitual reactions" and the latter "experience-dependent neuroplasticity.") (Goldstein) The sins of the fathers are visited upon the children; as you sow, so shall you reap; what goes around, comes around. Only grace and hard work can break the cycle.

Though the acute emotional distress of my depression is in remission, I still struggle with what the Desert Fathers and Mothers called *acedia*—what the Western Church has, as one of the "seven deadly sins," translated as "sloth," but is actually a deep spiritual lassitude that is a near relation to depression. It is always worse after a period of progress; Mother Theodora nailed it when she said, "You should realize that as soon as you intend to live in peace, at once evil comes and weighs down your soul through *acedia*, faint-heartedness, and evil thoughts." This is why the Desert Fathers and Mothers called *acedia* the Noonday Demon: it comes at mid-day to undermine all the resolve of the morning.

Toward the end of my university teaching period, I had a student who, because of what I had experienced myself, I was convinced was deeply depressed. The hole he couldn't climb out of was so familiar to me, I wished I could convey to him the fruit of my own struggle. It was terrifically frustrating knowing that some medication could have lifted the bell jar enough so he could breathe, allowing him to get out from under his feelings enough to take steps toward managing his thoughts. But in the end, he had to choose to do the work himself; no one could make him accept help.

Jesus couldn't. "Do you want to be well?" (John 5:6) he asked the paralyzed man at the pool—not, presumably, because he didn't know the answer, but because he needed the man to own the question. "Jerusalem, Jerusalem…again and again would I have taken your children to myself as a bird takes her young ones under her wings, and you would not!" (Matthew 23:37) And God can't force it on us either, or doesn't; we have to seek and accept the grace ourselves.

ⁱᵛ "The Noonday Demon" first appeared in *Elephant Journal* on June 25, 2011, in a much shorter form. Used here by permission.

-Chapter 2-

Welcome to the Real World

Though leaves are many, the root is one;
Through all the lying days of my youth
I swayed my leaves and flowers in the sun;
Now I may wither into the truth.
–W.B. Yeats, "The Coming of Wisdom with Time"

* * *

In the Wachowski Brothers' film *The Matrix*, sentient machines run the world. Human beings spend their lives curled up in tiny pods while the machines harvest their biochemical energy for power. All human experience—everything we see, hear, touch and taste on a daily basis, all our activity and our natural and man-made environments—is actually a computer-simulated illusion called the Matrix.

A cadre of revolutionaries resists the machines from their headquarters in the last human city on earth, a hidden underground stronghold called Zion. Life in Zion, outside the Matrix, is bleak, grey and dingy; food comes in the form of tasteless nutrient jelly, and there is a shabby, monochrome feeling to everything. In escaping the Matrix, the revolutionaries leave behind a world of comfortable illusion for a stark and forbidding reality. As their leader, a man known as Morpheus, tells them when they are recruited, "All I'm offering is the truth, nothing more."

But the inhabitants of Zion choose this dystopic reality over the comfortable and familiar computer-generated fiction of the Matrix. For many of them, the simulacrum never felt right; something was "off" in a way barely perceptible, and the illusory nature of the familiar lurked just beyond their peripheral vision. "Welcome to the real world," Morpheus tells them after their "extraction" from their pods.

A revolutionary named Cypher, having had all he could stand of the austere life outside the Matrix, betrays Morpheus to Agent Smith, an Artificial Intelligence program that, within the Matrix, appears as something similar to a Secret Service agent. In return for information that would lead him to Morpheus, Smith promises to have Cypher returned to his pod and hooked back into the Matrix, with all memory of the real world erased.

Before I was depressed, I thought I was happy. It's easy to look back at the time before everything fell apart and wish things could be that simple and satisfying again. But I know that the apparently pulled-together life I had before depression was an illusion, a paste-up, and that something in me always suspected as much. I had a lot more trouble with anger in the old days; now, I am more forgiving, more understanding. Before, I was much more invested in the goals my academic and social training had set before me; now I see more clearly what is really important, and what is right in front of me.

Some of those changes come with age, of course, but I think much of my mellowing is a gift of depression. Depression made my world less vivid, but less illusory, than before, and it has given me a greater ability to empathize, both with those who are still enthralled by the illusion, and with those who mourn it. And as tempting as it is sometimes to wish to return to the illusion, I know that if I were back in that world, I would never move forward, never grow spiritually; I would remain a slave to the passions and obsessions from which my depression was, in some sense, an escape. It is as if my subconscious mind rose up and said, Enough; I'm weary of being merely a power source for man-made things. I want the real world.

So I keep seeking, even though the first stage of my search has been troubling and disillusioning; I keep seeking, waiting for the astonishment to come—the astonishment Jesus promised to those who seek until they find.

Jesus said: The seeker should not stop seeking until he finds. When he finds, he will be disturbed. After being disturbed, he will be astonished. Then he will rule over all things. (Gospel of Thomas, Saying 2)

Chapter 3

Among the Deepening Shades

* * *

The elderly neighbor arrived at our house agitated, tearful, in a near-panic. Her husband was lying in the back yard, she told my mother. He had shot himself.

I was in middle school, and did not accompany the two women to the neighbor's yard. My mother later told us she had found him unconscious, his hands shaking like dry leaves. She held them until the ambulance arrived. He died shortly thereafter. Mowing the widow's lawn a few days later, I found the .22 caliber shell in the grass; it astonished me that so tiny a thing could end a life.

My mother explained to me that our neighbor had been "macho in his own skinny way," and was despondent over his increasing inability to manage his home, his large lawn and garden—his life. We had spent so many Christmas Eves by their fireside, so many summer afternoons on their screened-in porch, and never suspected that his age-related debilities were driving him to put an end to himself. To us, he had always seemed so vital, so hail-fellow-well-met. I wonder what kind of attention we would have needed to pay in order to see the signs that must surely have been there.

Attention must be paid, said Linda Loman in Arthur Miller's *Death of a Salesman*. A man may be a failure in his business like her husband Willy, or a retiree with no comforting prospect of his declining years like our neighbor, or immured in a nursing home out of even the minor tributaries, let alone the main stream, of life, and attention must nevertheless be paid to the old and out-of-it.

In my early twenties I was living in a cast house—a decommissioned church that had been converted into something like dormitories—with my fellow performers in an interactive theater troupe. The church was across the street from a retirement home, and three or four years running I dragged a few colleagues out of bed on a winter morning to go Christmas caroling around the home. As we were in the midst of the annual Dickens-themed Victorian Christmas show, we had a number of carols available to short-term memory. I brought my concertina, and we began singing in the dining room during lunch before roaming the decked halls, caroling at nurses' stations and in private rooms. Two residents in particular stand out in my memory.

The first is a wizened woman in a wheelchair who asked us if we knew "Stille Nacht"—a request not unusual in the Pennsylvania German belt. I did, as it turned out, and began to sing. I was only a few notes into the song when the woman clutched at the aide's sleeve, shouting "He knows it! He knows it!" before bursting—no, that is too puny a word—*erupting* into tears.

Good God, I thought; how long has it been since anyone has sung her favorite Christmas carol to this woman? Is no one part of her life enough to gratify so paltry a request?

The second is a bedridden woman with long, white hair worn loose and spreading over her pillow. Her name was Marie. Each year we gathered around her bed and sang, and she would sing along in nonsense sounds; the tune would be the same one we were singing, but without intelligible words. She sang robustly and seemed to enjoy herself, and we all assumed she was too demented to use language. (Being young and callow, we probably didn't even know what we meant by that.) Then the unforeseeable happened.

Several of us knew the old French carol, *"Il e né, le Divin enfant,"* and as we sang it, the woman sang along as always—but *in French*. Thunderstruck, one of us who spoke a little French struck up a halting conversation, and we discovered that far from being in a post-verbal dementia, she was, *au contraire*, very much intact mentally.

"Vous rencontrez un bon Noël?" our colleague asked Marie.

"No!" Marie replied with a petulant shake of the head.

"Quelle est votre idée d'un bon Noël?" The old woman smiled and laid her feather-light hand on my friend's.

"Une chanteuse!" she replied.

Re-entering the room, the nurse explained that Marie, who was French-Canadian and spoke no English, had toured with a vaudeville troupe in her youth, singing and playing the ukulele. "She loved music!" she kept saying, with a patronizing smile. ("It sounds like she still does," one of us ventured, to no apparent effect.) Marie had no living family or friends, and no one in the home spoke French. I cannot imagine living in that kind of isolation and not coming unhinged. And while Marie's situation was certainly an outlier—and far less likely to occur today than a quarter century ago—a lot of older people, even in much less extreme circumstances, find life not worth the effort.

By the middle of this decade, 13 percent of Americans were elderly—but that 13 percent committed almost a fifth of the nation's suicides. The National Institute of Mental Health (NIMH) has identified major depression as the biggest risk factor in late-life suicides. (NIMH)

But in a 2004 NIMH study, the simple addition of "depression care managers"—social workers, nurses and psychologists who coordinated and followed up on the care of depressed elderly residents—led to a dramatic improvement in patient ideation. Eight months into the study, "about 70 percent of intervention patients initially plagued by suicidal thoughts were free of them, compared to about 44 percent of 'usual care' patients." (NIMH)

Because the actual care the managers provided was determined in part by their area of expertise and in part by patient preferences, it seems likely that it was primarily their caring presence, rather than any specific therapeutic interventions, that made the difference. Andrew Solomon seems to have hit the nail on the head: "Old people feel better when more attention is paid to them." (Solomon, *The Noonday Demon: An Atlas of Depression*)

Another NIMH study from 2008 showed that the subject of mental health only came up in 22 percent of elderly people's visits with their primary care physicians, and in those visits, only two minutes out of an average of 16 were given to the subject. In many cases, doctors dismissed patients' mental health concerns without follow-up. (NIMH)

Of course, the etiology of depression is more complicated than simple neglect; depression in the elderly can also be caused by a loss of blood supply to the brain as a result of vascular disease—and in those patients, antidepressants like selective serotonin reuptake inhibitors (SSRIs) are less effective. (NIMH) Still, it is interesting that Jesus didn't include the elderly among "the least of these" in His story of the sheep and the goats; (Matthew 25:31-46) apparently, respect for the aged was taken enough for granted in ancient Israel that a sentence like "I was elderly, and you paid attention to me" would have sounded downright strange.

I did a stint of clinical pastoral training at a Continuing Care Retirement Community (CCRC) that is one of the best in the country. After making my regular rounds in the health care center, I spent much of my time doing what my supervisor, the community's chaplain, called "loitering with intention"—hanging around the large lobby area that served as the "town square" and striking up conversations with people. Some seemed to be thriving—taking advantage of craft classes, bus trips to concerts, theater or shopping, attending lectures and "chair aerobics" in the auditorium, playing bridge in the many small common areas, and participating in the community's religious activities.

But as often as not, sadness enveloped the people I talked with: a resigned determination not to be a burden to their children, cultivated in the face of their infrequent contact with them; grief over the loss of a spouse; the pain of trading old homes, neighborhoods and possessions for the community's relatively small apartments—all the changes and chances attendant on moving into a retirement community after a lifetime of independence. "I wouldn't say I'm exactly 'happy,'" one woman told me in a voice tinged with regret. "You could say I'm...content."

When I wasn't visiting the sick or chatting people up in the lobby, I was in the library poring over the biographical sketches in the community's photo-directory. I found that almost without exception, the residents had grown up more engaged with their communities than subsequent generations have been; most of the men were veterans, and many belonged to fraternal and service organizations, while the women piloted a large array of civic, religious and charitable groups. As I learned more about the residents' former lives, it became clear to me why the community sponsored so many well-attended social events—and why, notwithstanding, so many of the residents seemed lonely and sad.

Why do some of those who have aged out of the wider public square thrive while others deteriorate? Why do some stay socially engaged while others become socially isolated? What is standing in the way of people enjoying their increasingly protracted "golden years"? It is tempting to blame the effects of aging themselves, but I think that is a cop-out. I have seen older people with a wide range of physical and mental abilities and disabilities continue to contribute to their communities well into their "declining years," while others seem to grow old before their time. Barring seriously debilitating conditions like Alzheimer's disease, becoming a little dotty needn't stand in the way of doing things and being happy.

I knew a woman who was a pillar of the Jewish community in her retirement village. Not a holiday or event went by that she wasn't in the middle of, making arrangements, reaching out to the less active, and providing motive power by the sheer force of her benignly officious enthusiasm. One day she came to the chaplain's office to apologize for not having signed up for the upcoming Seder celebration; some relatives whom she seldom got to see were going to be in town, she explained, and while she truly regretted not being at the community observance, she needed to spend time with her family. The chaplain thanked her for the notice, as well as all her work in getting the banquet together, and assured her that she understood. Wishing the energetic old woman a happy visit with her family, the chaplain closed the office door, then leaned against it, shaking with laughter.

"That's the third time she's been in here to tell me that!" she said.

When my mom was dying of cancer, she began giving me her books (which I had long been in the habit of "borrowing" anyway) saying that she didn't have enough time left to finish them herself. (While she didn't add that she didn't want to spend the time she did have reading books, I suspect that was true also.) I am fast approaching the age at which my mom died, and as I get older, I find an increasing urgency to read and learn as much as I can. I'm not sure whether I'm trying to "prepare" myself for whatever comes next, or to distract myself from the increasing stiffness of my aging body and mind. Probably some of both. Probably, like Yeats, I'm trying to provision my inner world as a bunker against the ravages of the dissolutions that are coming to us all along "among the deepening shades."[7]

---

[7] Yeats, W.B. "The Tower"

-Chapter 4-

The Indweller[v]

The marvelous world of thoughts, sensation, emotions, and inspiration, the spectacular world of creation around us, are all patterns of stunning weather on the holy mountain of God. But we are not the weather. We are the mountain. —Martin Laird, *Into the Silent Land*

* * *

"Thank you very much for coming today."

"My pleasure, Bobbi. Would you like to stay here in your room, or shall I wheel you back into the common room?"

(Long pause)

"I don't know what the difference is."

We in the West struggle with the Buddhist concept of no-self. The idea that there is no *person* in us—no lasting reality to our thoughts, feelings, and personality—doesn't sit well with us; it seems atheistic and nihilist. We infer that it means we are, at bottom, nothing but chemicals—a "bag of dirty water on legs." (Pratchett, *Wintersmith* 332) This is probably due to misunderstanding of the doctrine by a culture, Judeo-Christian in its thought patterns, that centralizes the immortality of the "soul"—by which it means the individual, determined personality. Even people who do not walk any organized spiritual path, and who have experienced the falling away of much of what we think of as the "soul," sense that

...you are never the same once you have acquired the knowledge that there is no self that will not crumble. We are told to learn self-reliance, but it's tricky if you have no self on which to rely...I am no spiritualist and I grew up without religion, but that ropy fiber that runs through the center of me, that holds fast even when the self has been stripped away from it: anyone who lives through this knows that it is never as simple as complicated chemistry. (Solomon 47)

Fred lays inert with eyes closed in the reclining hospital chair that takes up about half the available floor space in his retirement-home room. I have gone through the Administration of Communion service without any idea if he has heard anything. Because he is incapable of receiving the bread, I wet his lips with a few drops of the wine.

Although I cherish the belief that his spirit has benefited from the ritual even if his mind is unaware of it, I do not know exactly what I mean by that; in fact, I fear just the opposite. If a person's mind is gone, isn't that person gone, too?

If emotions, cognition and memory are all at the mercy of events, liable to physical insult and vulnerable to disease, what does it mean to say that the soul is immortal? When the personality is lost or damaged, what becomes of the person?

Science tells us that the mind is physically determined, a machine made of chemicals and neurons. This is science's rationale, for instance, for allowing a person in a persistent vegetative state to die: if all that makes a person a person is broken, what remains is just an empty shell.

Was Terri Schiavo's soul imprisoned in her irretrievably damaged body during her last fifteen years, or did it flee when everything identifiable as "Terri Schiavo" was destroyed? After she collapsed in 1990 from cardiac arrest brought on by bulimia, her doctors informed her family that she was in a persistent vegetative state. Her husband, believing that she would not wish to be kept alive artificially with no hope of recovery, petitioned to have her feeding tube removed. Her parents, against all medical evidence, maintained that their daughter was conscious, and fought to keep her on life support in a battle that ultimately involved Congress and President George W. Bush. Her artificial life support was finally terminated in 2005.

Judging by the hysteria among conservative Christians over her fate, Terri Schiavo was still "in there," and allowing her to die amounted to murder. But interestingly, the furor didn't center around there being more to a person than the cognitive faculties—rather, the opposition focused on arguing that those faculties were, all evidence to the contrary notwithstanding, still intact. In effect, the conservatives validated the assumptions of science by arguing that Schiavo ought to be kept alive, not because brainstuff isn't all there is to a human being, but because Schiavo's brainstuff was still working. Even when the autopsy showed a brain shrunken to half its normal size, and proved that the eyes that had supposedly followed moving objects were in fact blind, the conservatives continued to assert that these facts had been falsified by the shadowy agents of our alleged "culture of death."

Foolish and deluded? Of course. And yet, most of us find it difficult to believe that our thoughts and emotions are not our essential selves, but simply a function of our physical bodies.

My mother died of breast cancer that metastasized throughout her body, including her brain. Toward the end, as her mind became increasingly effected, I began to feel as though I were on a Tilt-a-Whirl—that now-old-fashioned amusement park ride in which each rider stands upright in a little niche on a large disk, the whole of which rotates until someone throws up. It seemed as though I shared the ride with a great many people from my mother's life, while she stood in the center and spoke to whomever was opposite her when the ride stopped. Sometimes she would begin a sentence addressing me, and end it addressing her prom date, or someone else I couldn't see.

During this period I picked up a copy of Charles Dickens's *Life and Adventures of Nicholas Nickleby,* and got as far as the eighth chapter. Nicholas has been sent to work in one of the horrible Yorkshire boarding schools where unwanted boys were sent to get them out of the way. He befriends a young man named Smike who has been there longer than all the other boys, and who, his family having stopped payment and disappeared long ago, has functioned for years as an abused drudge for the family who owns the school. The cringing boy tells Nicholas why he lives without hope.

> *'Do you remember the boy that died here?'*
> *'I was not here, you know,' said Nicholas gently; 'but what of him?'*
> *...'I was with him at night, and when it was all silent he cried no more for friends he wished to come and sit with him, but began to see faces round his bed that came from home; he said they smiled, and talked to him; and he died at last lifting his head to kiss them. Do you hear?'*
> *'Yes, yes,' rejoined Nicholas.*
> *'What faces will smile on me when I die!' cried his companion, shivering. 'Who will talk to me in those long nights! They*

cannot come from home; they would frighten me, if they did, for I don't know what it is, and shouldn't know them. Pain and fear, pain and fear for me, alive or dead. No hope, no hope!'

Though my mother spent her last illness, as she had spent her life, surrounded by family and friends, the similarity between her—hallucinations? visitations?—and those of the boy of whom Smike told Nicholas was too eerie for me to handle at the time. I put the book down, and didn't pick it up again for fifteen years. But the question remained: what is going on in the consciousness of people with one foot in this world and one in the next? And do the disturbances in the consciousness and perceptions of the dying—whether lively, as with my mother, or comatose, as with Fred—have any effect upon, or communion with, the essential self that lies beneath mind and personality?

In Yogic thought, both the intellect and our emotions are part of our physical equipment, and neither has any effect whatever on our essential selves. The Purusha, or "indweller," is unchanging, and only appears to take on our mental states as a clear crystal seems to take on the color of objects close by. While the "mind is an instrument, as it were, in the hands of the Soul, through which the Soul perceives external objects," (Vivekananda, *Raja Yoga* 82) the Purusha/Soul itself is unaffected by the experiences of the mind.

The Purusha does not love; It is love itself. It does not exist; It is existence itself. The Soul does not know; It is knowledge itself. It is a mistake to say that the Soul loves, exists, or knows. Love, existence, and knowledge are not the qualities of the Purusha, but Its essence...the great Atman, the Infinite Being, without birth or death, established in Its own glory. (Vivekananda, *Raja Yoga* 138)

While it may seem radical for a Christian to speak of the Atman, the "universal soul" which is identical both with the individual purusha and Brahman/God, other Christians have gone there—or at least nearby—before. Thomas Aquinas (who was considered a radical—even a heretic—in his day, but quickly became the go-to guy for the institutional church) believed that the soul survives the body as an individual personality, but that it doesn't start out that way.

The soul is capable of surviving on its own, but it does not inhabit the body like a "ghost in the machine." On the contrary, it is only by uniting with a human body that it becomes individualized, obtaining an identity that persists even after the body dies. Imagine some material, like molten metal, poured into a mold to make a sculpture. When the mold is broken, the metal survives, but it owes its permanent shape to the experience of being in the mold. What survives, in the case of human beings, is not some abstract, depersonalized soul, but the form of a real individual person. (Rubinstein 213)

This model is similar to the Yogic doctrine that the samskaras, or "impressions" imposed upon the mind by our actions, survive the body and persist into subsequent incarnations. But Yoga also posits that the "mind" is part of the physical body, and dies with it, while the samskaras remain as the "seeds" of future karma.

And while the Schiavo protesters may have been unaware of it, Christian as well as Yogic thought has long urged against identifying ourselves with our thoughts, feelings and memories. These things are not our essential selves, which are unchanging, imperishable, rooted in the divine.

That "fundamental truth of our union with God"

(Laird 10) is the first liberating truth I learned from Yoga— for while the principle has been present in Christian thought from the beginning, it is not emphasized, so I had to hear of it in the "foreign language" of Yoga in order to recognize it in my own tradition.

The idea that we are already one with God would scandalize many contemporary Christians, especially in the Reformed churches, which tend to regard humanity as fundamentally estranged from God in our "total depravity."[8] What they think Jesus meant when He said, "I am the Vine, you are the branches" (John 15:5) is beyond me; it's not like the two are made of different stuff. But it took the Yogic principle that our job is not to *effect* our union with God, but to *realize* it, to make me see that.

In his letter to the Christians in Thessalonika, the Apostle Paul seems to distinguish between our physical, mental/emotional, and essential selves:

May your whole spirit, soul and body be kept blameless at the coming of our Lord Jesus Christ. (1 Thessalonians 5:23 ESV)

While the meaning of this passage has been disputed for centuries, I subscribe to the theory that Paul's word *psychí*, translated as "soul", refers to the transient stuff of which our individual personalities are constituted, while *pneuma*, or "spirit," refers to the imperishable, essential nature—in Zen Buddhist terms, the "Self-nature" that is not born with this incarnation. (Wu 55)

The fact that "soul" is almost always used in reference to mortals and not to God, for Whom the word "spirit" is always used, confirms me in this belief. But what

---

[8] A key doctrine of Calvinism.

29

really brought this realization home to me was the Yogic doctrine of the "Self", or Divine essence at our core, and the "self", or the "small" identity made up of our thoughts, feelings and memories.

I believe that when Jesus described Himself as "the Way, the Truth and the Life," He referred not to incidentals—the name and form of a carpenter from Nazareth—but to essentials: the Divine Being that transcends all biography. Not the weather, but the mountain; not His self, but HimSelf—which is also our Self.

And I believe that when I give Communion to someone no longer able to receive it under their own power, that it bypasses the defunct self and goes straight for the immortal Self of that person. And that while the death of the body means the end of the self, it is merely a new beginning for the Self.

There is a Zen Buddhist exercise in which one repeatedly asks, "Who am I?" and then replies, to each answer that presents itself, "That is not who I am." All those answers have to do with what the Yogis call *nama* and *rupa*—Sanskrit for "name" and "form"—not essential reality. I believe nama and rupa, which the Yogis regard as contingent and evanescent, are the "life in this world" that Jesus calls us to hold lightly, so that the eternal life can live itself in us now.

Those who love their life in this world will lose it. Those who care nothing for their life in this world will keep it for eternal life. (John 12:25)

ᵛ This chapter originally appeared under the title "The Three Most Liberating Things I Have Learned From Yoga, Part 1" in *Elephant*

Journal on February 9, 2011, in slightly different form. Used here by permission.

-Chapter 5-

Willy Loman's Front Stoop[vi]

Vocation, the way I was seeking it, becomes an act of will, a grim determination that one's life will go this way or that whether it wants to or not. –Parker Palmer, *Let Your Life Speak*

Misery comes through attachment, not through work. As soon as we identify ourselves with the work we do, we feel miserable; but if we do not identify ourselves with it, we do not feel that misery. –Swami Vivekananda, *Karma Yoga*

* * *

During a delusional period when I was pursuing what I thought was a vocation to the ordained Christian ministry, someone gave me a list of things ordination would *not* do. Two items on the list were:

1. It will not make you more holy.
2. It will not make you less lonely.

Preparing to self-identify as clergy will improve neither your interior make-up nor your social situation. And why should it? We can practice Christian ministry without being ordained ministers; in fact, all Christians are called upon to do just that. But as a colleague of mine put it at the time, "People get to a certain level of holiness, and they think they ought to be ordained." The same, of course, goes for other traditions; you can practice yoga without needing to self-identify as a yogi. A mala around your wrist won't make you any more holy than a clerical collar around your neck.

But people feel a strong need to identify themselves as something—to deploy social markers that, they believe, will make them feel more (or at least appear more) holy, sexy, smart, successful, wealthy, important, sophisticated, stylish, influential or any combination of the above.

For ten years, my university teaching job functioned as an identity, a shield against imposter syndrome. Whenever I was feeling inadequate, or in danger of being treated dismissively, I could always stand on my dignity as an *academic*. The fact that leading people in a folk music sing-along made me happier than what I did in academia was irrelevant; when people encouraged me to go on the performing circuit, I'd assure them that folk music (which I loved) was only a hobby; classical music (about which I had easy-to-ignore misgivings) was my *vocation*.

I never wrote more music, or had more success in the classical music world in which I was trained, than when I worked on a loading dock. I'd get home at 3:30, take a shower, and compose music all afternoon and evening. (And I could lift heavy things.) But I spent an awful lot of that period of my life being miserable. Given the opportunity to be a working class sage like the garbage man in Dilbert, or Larry Darrell in *The Razor's Edge*, I squandered it bitching and moaning about "wasting my life." *I am a composer*, I kept telling myself, as though the fact that I spent several hours every day composing had no bearing on that fact. And maybe going back to school and getting a teaching job were the right things to do, and maybe they weren't. I do know that I wasn't as "successful" a composer as an adjunct professor as I was when I was working in a tire warehouse; I was only marginally less miserable.

Death of a Salesman is the story of Willy Loman, a traveling rep who never makes the splash in the world that he wants to. Though he makes a living, he never becomes the successful, universally known and "well-liked" figure he desperately wants to be. Moreover, his son Biff, having rejected his father's profession, is also failing to make something of himself, in Willy's estimation. Ultimately, Willy attempts to redeem his own failure by committing suicide in order to finance a business for his sons with the life insurance money.

After Willy's death, Biff tries to get his still gung-ho younger brother Happy to see the truth about their father. Though Willy had put his whole life into succeeding as a salesman, Biff argues that his true calling was masonry, which Willy regarded as a mere hobby. "There is more of him in that front stoop than in all the sales he ever made," Biff says, referring to one of Willy's projects. "He had the wrong dreams. All, all wrong."

How does a person travel down the wrong road for years, decades—even a whole lifetime? Is there no voice within saying, "Wait, stop, go back, exit here"? And if there is, how do we silence it, and why? Like the man who looked for hours under a streetlight for the keys he had dropped in the alley because the light was better there, we waste so much time looking for what we want where it isn't to be found, consumed by "the underlying fear of... being torn away from our chosen image of what or who we are in this world." (Miller)

This is when the depression—which had, I believe, been crouching at the door most of my life, and had begun to manifest itself after the birth of my first daughter—launched its full-bore assault: when, having quit my teaching job, I no longer had that "chosen image" to identify with.

And what I was told about becoming ordained Christian clergy was also true of becoming ordained Interfaith clergy: while it's something I love doing, it isn't something I can *be* to the exclusion, augmentation, or justification of just being myself. It has made me neither more holy nor less lonely. And it does nothing to erase the pain of having spent so much on all the wrong dreams.

But here's what it does do—besides allowing me to minister to people pastorally and ritually/sacramentally. I'll illustrate with a story.

During my ill-conceived run at Christian ordination, I had a conversation with one of my parish priests about my dislike of clerical collars. I'd be afraid, I told her, that people would become self-conscious and police their behavior and language around someone in a dog collar. (Note: it ain't necessarily so.) She acknowledged that possibility, but told me about the day before when she had gone to a coffee shop in her clericals. Being a Dead Head from way back, she complimented the barista on his elaborately tie-dyed t-shirt. He was surprised to hear such a compliment from a woman in a clerical collar, and they had a spirited conversation about All Things Dead.

By wearing her collar, she explained, she had been able to open up that young man's mind—through their shared enthusiasm for the Grateful Dead—to the full humanity of one clergy person and, by extension, to a church he might have expected to be indifferent at best, and censorious at worst, toward things he cared about.

As inconsequential as this incident may seem (and who can say what its consequences actually were?) I have learned, many years later, how applicable the principle is to many situations. For example, an old friend and fellow Third Order Franciscan is living out the unusually paired vocations of police detective and Episcopal deacon. (Deacons are ordained clergy who, unlike parish priests who must spend a lot of time on administrative work, concentrate their ministry on direct service to those in need. See Acts 6:1-7.) While most police officers, my friend tells me, are atheists, he has applied an old-fashioned neighborhood policing technique to his diaconal ministry: he and his supervising priest walk a "beat" through the streets of the very poor, blighted and drug-infested neighborhood in which their church is situated. They greet their neighbors, shake their hands, learn their names, and develop the trusting relationships that beat cops used to have with the people they served before the militarization of law enforcement took the police off the sidewalks and hunkered them down in squad cars. (Balko) The mutual respect that community policing used to build between the uniformed officer and the citizenry, my friend is now building between the uniformed clergy and those who live and struggle in the shadow of his church's steeple and within the sound of its bells.

I have experienced this phenomenon myself as well. The night the St. Louis, Missouri grand jury declined to indict Darren Wilson in the Ferguson death of Michael Brown, a call went out from Philadelphians Organized to Witness, Empower and Rebuild (POWER) for all available clergy to assemble at a Center City Philadelphia church to craft a statement to be read before joining the planned protest march. "Wear clericals," the announcement said.

After writing the statement, we moved to the sidewalk outside City Hall, where one of POWER's clergy leaders read the document before news cameras.

"Clergy in front, please!" shouted a voice as we moved from City Hall into the street to join the march. By making the clerical leadership as visible as possible, we hoped not only to lend to the cause of racial justice whatever weight and authority clergy may still wield, but also to counteract the widespread (and largely inaccurate) image of the churches as indifferent or hostile to social activism.

POWER also helped organize the #ReclaimMLKDay march in 2015, and my own parish contributed some thirty marchers to the event. As I carried a sign demanding a livable minimum wage, I saw many eyes move from the sign to my collar, followed by a smile or thumbs-up. "Thank you for coming, Father," said one young woman as we approached the Constitution Center.

The difference, I think, between identifying as an academic and identifying as clergy—for me, anyway—is that the first merely kept terror and dislocation at bay, whilst the latter makes me actively happy. I believe this has less to do with the work itself—I could have made my teaching less of a "day job" and more of a ministry if I'd wanted to—than with the use I have made of the identifying role.

I have said that I used the label "academic" as a shield, a protective barrier between the harsh world and my fragile ego, keeping my insecurities and sublimated low-level panic out of the light. My "clergy" label, on the other hand, I use as a tool in the service of that same world and, through it, of that world's Creator. Rather than proclaiming (as I thought) my worthiness and importance, it allows me to act as a lay figure, modeling God's love for the world. It has taken the focus off me as a paste-up of self-touted talents and accomplishments and redirected it toward the One Who only requires of us that we "do justice, love mercy, walk humbly with our God." (Micah 6:8) And that is how holiness in brought into the world, loneliness assuaged, true identity established, and the sword of depression refashioned into the ploughshare of service and love.

[vi] A version of this chapter first appeared under the title "Who Do You Think You Are?" at RecoveringYogi.com on February 10, 2012, in slightly different form. Used here by permission.

-Chapter 6-

Eating My Money[vii]

> ...*I am in blood*
> *Stepped in so far that should I wade no more,*
> *Returning were as tedious as go o'er.*
> –William Shakespeare, *MacBeth*, Act III, Scene 4

* * *

Mullah Nasruddin[9] spent a long day traveling by donkey, and by late afternoon was famished and very thirsty.

He met a man selling what looked like juicy, delicious fruit, and paid everything in his purse for the whole basket. Upon closer examination, he realized that he had bought not fruit, but hot peppers.

Some miles later, one of his neighbors saw him, choking down one hot pepper after another, eyes streaming and sweat pouring off him.

"Mullah, what are you doing?" the distressed acquaintance asked. "Why are you eating all those hot peppers?"

"I'm not eating hot peppers," the mullah replied; "I'm eating my money."

About halfway through my doctoral studies in music

---

[9] Mullah Nasruddin stories are told all over the Islamic world. I heard this particular one from Ted Richards at a retreat with the New Seminary for Interfaith Studies.

I came within a whisker of quitting. There just didn't seem to be any point to getting a degree in classical music composition. But I decided to tough it out; since I already had the debt, I figured, I might as well get the degree. So I ate my money.

In a way, the degree was only the last pepper in the basket. Ever since childhood, my real loves had been folk and devotional music; I had always preferred "singing with" to "singing to." But for some reason that therapy has not yet been able to ferret out, I was convinced that the music I loved to make was merely avocational—that my true calling was to the more "significant" world of concert music. So without any spectacular talent, by dint of hard work and a good ear, I choked down those peppers for a long time.

Of course, if I hadn't finished the degree, I'd never have had 10 years of university teaching work; if I had gone on the road as a folk musician, I'd never have met my splendid wife nor had my wonderful children. So I'm not presuming to know better than whatever karmic forces may or may not have been influencing my life decisions. But I can't help wondering what life would have been like had I listened to the healthy part of my heart rather than the diseased part, and pursued what really made me happy rather than what I had, for some reason, decided was "legitimate." I sometimes think a conversation like this one (from Somerset Maugham's *Of Human Bondage*), put into musical rather than painting terms, might have been the best thing that could have happened to me:

"You have a certain manual dexterity. With hard work and perseverance there is no reason why you should not become a careful, not incompetent painter...I see no talent in anything you have shown me. I see industry and intelligence. You will never be anything but

mediocre."...

Monsieur Foinet got up and made as if to go, but he changed his mind and, stopping, put his hand on Philip's shoulder.

"But if you were to ask me my advice, I should say: take your courage in both hands and try your luck at something else. It sounds very hard, but let me tell you this: I would give all I have in the world if someone had given me that advice when I was your age and I had taken it."

Now, if I were the only one who, having taken a wrong turn, ignored both personal discomfort and external evidence while barreling all the faster down the wrong path, there would be no need for stories like the one I began with. But the mullah represents a very widespread and familiar pattern of human behavior.

Why is it so hard to change course? Are we in the grip of Stockholm Syndrome to "the devil we know"? We make decisions about ourselves, and our identities harden around them. If change does come, or threatens to, we fear it and romanticize the past —no matter how miserable the past really was. "Were there not enough graves in Egypt, that you have brought us to die in the wilderness?" the Israelites asked Moses at the Sea of Reeds. "Better a slave in Egypt than a corpse in the desert!" (Exodus 14:11-12)

Sometimes these decisions are based on "shoulds" and "oughts." For years, I filled my music collection with "classics" I believed that I, as a classically trained musician, "ought" to have in my collection. (Some of them I actually listened to, and still do.) It wasn't until, in the throes of a midlife crisis, I quit my teaching job, that I was able to fill a garbage can with CDs I didn't care about and devote myself to the music I actually like.

While misplaced loyalty to the should and oughts

with which we grow up, and the dissonance between what we believe we should value and what we actually do, can keep us beating for years on a dead horse, there are other ways in which depression short-circuits our ability to take stock of our lives and to do what is necessary to change them. One, perhaps surprisingly, is that it reduces our emotional reactivity.

Strong emotions are motivators to change. Anger drives us to repel its object; fear drives us to flee what frightens us; happiness tells us we are doing things right. Our minds marshal our emotions in response to events; that is their purpose. In depression, however, the relationship between what happens and how we feel is broken; we experience a reduced range of emotions, and emotional inertia sets in. (Kuppens, Allen, Nicholas B. and Sheeber, Lisa) We come to believe that nothing we do will make any difference, and this belief both causes, and is triggered by, a reduction in the diversity of emotional responses that prompt us to make changes.

But there's another side to this. Before I was actively depressed—by which I mean that the malaise with which I had been living for many years, perhaps even most of my life, came out of the shadows and shut everything down—I was triumphant when things "worked out," angry, frustrated and sad when they didn't. I was at the mercy of events, emotionally. In the grip of depression, nothing seemed to matter enough to get worked up about. The advantage of this is that I was no longer tossed about emotionally by events; the disadvantage was that I lacked the emotional horsepower to change anything. (This is one of the reasons that some therapists encourage anger in their patients suffering from abuse-related depressive conditions like Complex Post-Traumatic Stress Disorder; besides moving the patient's loathing from the self to the abuser, anger can be a powerful driver for change.) (Walker 122)

Finally, I believe a major reason why we ignore the inner promptings of the soul is fear—which may be part of the reason that Jesus said, "Do not be afraid" more than any other single recorded thing. If we do things differently, our lives will change—and that's scary once we've gotten cozy with the devil we know.

"Fear," said Pema Chödrön, "is a natural reaction to moving closer to the truth." It almost seems as though we would rather regret having never met ourselves than go through the ordeal of the meeting; many of us—especially, I'd argue, those in the grip of untreated depression—would rather just go on eating the peppers. We're frightened, we're running on reduced emotional resources, and we're invested in the way we do things. In the absence of some motivating crisis, cutting our losses and chucking the peppers is just more than many of us can face.

---

vii A shorter version of this chapter first appeared under the title "Staying the Course" in *Elephant Journal* on July 10, 2012. Used here by permission.

Chapter 7

Letting Down the Nets

Once you have built something - something that takes all your passion and will - it becomes more precious to you than your own happiness. You don't realise that, while you are building it. That you are creating a martyrdom - something which, later, will make you suffer. –Sofia Samatar, *A Stranger in Olondria*

* * *

On a family vacation—I must have been ten or eleven—I remember fishing off the end of a pier with a bobber and a night crawler, catching assorted respectable but unremarkable pan fish. On the same dock was a man casting a spoon lure out into the deeper water—and he was catching silver bass. I asked him why I wasn't catching silver bass. "Because you ain't fishing for 'em," he replied.

I got an early start fishing for one thing and being disappointed at not catching another. Once my mind is set on a particular course, I find it almost impossible to see things in any other way, to imagine any other possibilities. I'm not alone in this, of course; most of us are very good at sticking to the stories we tell ourselves about ourselves.

There are probably many reasons why we do this. Sometimes it's the attendant ordeal that militates against change, the arduousness of starting afresh. In Kevin Smith's 1997 film *Chasing Amy*, Holden (played by Ben Affleck) tells Alyssa (played by Joey Lauren Adams) that he is in love with her—that he can no longer sustain their straight man/lesbian friendship, which has become too painful for him. Alyssa, who has fiercely self-identified with lesbian sexuality, becomes furious.

She walks away. Holden stands there, at a loss. Then he turns and heads back to his car.

As he reaches the door and turns to look back at her, Alyssa pounces on him, grabs his face and locks lips with him, big time. He drops his keys and embraces her.

And there they stand, by the side of the road, drenched, kissing.

Alyssa's fury, of course, is not due so much to the perceived affront to her sexuality, which is obviously more complicated than she wanted to believe, as to the affront to her self-constructed *identity*. Acknowledging her feelings for Holden would be like trying to turn a barge around in a brisk current. She has too much momentum going the other way.

But if we sometimes avoid change because of the difficulties it would cause, I think we also avoid it out of a failure of imagination—an inability to see what part of what we're doing isn't working.

Before we were married, my wife worked on a schooner for eight months. She had grown up around boats, and generally knew what she was doing. But one windy day in the Virgin Islands it fell to her to take a group of tourists ashore in the tender—the small boat that ferries passengers and crew between the ship and the shore. She had never done this with the sea as rough as it was that day, and the boat became swamped as she approached the beach. As she and the passengers attempted to haul the boat ashore, the incoming waves kept coming in over the stern and pulling the boat back out to sea. After several unsuccessful attempts to land, she heard a West Indian man, who was watching from the shore, shout "Turn de boat aroun', mon!" So she did—and when the boat presented its pointed bow to the sea, the oncoming waves had nothing to grab on to, and pilot and passengers were able to land and drain the boat.

In retrospect, turning the boat around seems an elegantly simple solution, but committed as she was to the course she had planned, it just never occurred to her. ("Her prior experience having been limited to pointing the boat where she wanted it go," she adds over my shoulder.)

Sometimes we're afraid of what will happen if the new course succeeds where the familiar old one is failing— it might change everything forever, and we're not sure we can handle that:

(Jesus) said to Simon, "Put out into the deep water and let down your nets for a catch." Simon answered, "Master, we've worked hard all night and haven't caught anything. But because you say so, I will let down the nets." When they had done this, they caught so many fish that their nets were beginning to break. So they signaled their partners in the other boat to come and help them. And they came and filled both boats, so that they began to sink. But when Simon Peter saw it, he fell down at Jesus' knees, saying, "Go away from me, Lord, for I am a sinful man!" For amazement had seized him and all his companions because of the catch of fish which they had taken. (Luke 5:1-9 NIV)

There is a great catch lurking in the depths, and we are afraid of it. We get so adept at neutralizing the inner voice that urges us to change. We may not silence it entirely, but we can render it ineffective.

One of my early dates with my wife was a visit to the Brandywine River Museum in Chadd's Ford,

Pennsylvania, which houses a large collection of paintings by the Wyeths. As we browsed the gift shop, looking at prints of Andrew Wyeth landscapes in their solemn greys and browns, she showed me how, by turning the picture upside-down, you could get a better idea of the actual palette. I was shocked as greens, reds, and purples I hadn't seen before popped out of the inverted picture. My eye had been so seduced by the form, the referent scene signified by the painting, that it had seen only the colors it expected the represented objects to be. Upside down, the form became incomprehensible, freeing my eye to see the hues that were actually before it.

I have learned a lot about myself since walking away from my self-constructed identity of composer-academic. I have learned that I love doing sacred ministry, that hospice chaplaincy is extraordinarily satisfying to me, that singing my music with an audience gives me more of a charge than engaging someone else to sing it to them ever could. I've also learned how entrenched I am in bad habits, how un-mindful and neglectful of the here-and-now I can be, and how dependent I am upon externally imposed structure. And all these colors have always been there, integral to the picture that is me, even when obscured by the form.

You may have heard that the Chinese characters comprising the Mandarin word for "crisis" literally translate as "danger-opportunity." When life turns us upside down, taking away from us the form into which we have cast ourselves, it is just such a crisis: we can be paralyzed by depression and anxiety, stuck in a drab, mud-colored world—that's the danger—or we can reassess our true colors. Therein lies the opportunity. It takes courage to seize it—and treatment, and grace, and loving support—but what a revelation, when the colors we didn't know were there leap out of the blackness like flashing silver fish being hauled up from the dark depths.

-Chapter 8-

The Treasures of Darkness[viii]

I will give you the treasures of darkness and riches hidden in secret places, so that you may know that I am the Lord, the God of Israel, who summons you by name. —Isaiah 45:3

* * *

When I was younger, I seasoned everything I ate with hot pepper. It was strong and stimulating, and it hurt so good. But as I got older, I became less able to tolerate the onslaught. My mouth still craved it, but the rest of me could no longer stand it.

As time went on, my palette recalibrated and I discovered that I had long been missing out on myriad subtle flavors because I had been overwhelming them with capsaicin. I developed an appreciation for palatal nuance and learned to pay closer attention to the play of flavors in my food.

Depression did a similar thing to me. During the many years when it was percolating below the surface, my emotional life was like a big bottle of Sriracha, a piquant sauce of anger and frustration, resentment and near-panic slathered all over everything. All red-hot, all the time. Now, the emotional flavors are more complex; I am aware of subtler shades of feeling. Some, like sadness and shame, I used to purposely drown out with the sauce; others, like tenderness, and the acute awareness of the passing of time that parenthood imparts, have both emerged from under the salsa and been augmented by my own maturation.

In addition to undifferentiated emotional piquancy, I find that there is a certain kind of moral hot sauce of the soul that cripples our sense of ethical subtlety and nuance, and that it is generally in greater supply when we are young. As a callow youth I was inordinately self-righteous, quick to judge and to take sides, incredibly slow to repent, always ready to find an excuse for anything I did. I wince when I think of those days.

I think it's normal to grow in tolerance for human frailty as one gains experience; the more we see of life, the harder it becomes to assume we know the whole story. But I wonder what faculties are actually altered by exposure to life—what about us changes as we develop a broader perspective?

If we conceive of the moral universe in a charts-and-tables way based on abstractions about "right" and "wrong," surely that system would remain untouched by the passage of time. But what if increasing maturity reframes the subject, bringing different faculties to bear like taste buds shaking off their Tabasco-induced stupor? What if growing up makes us available to subtleties of feeling?

I believe that most of our decisions are, at bottom, aesthetic decisions—including those we might ordinarily categorize as moral. In his *Ethics*, Aristotle makes the startling but compelling claim that no one can be called truly virtuous who does not take pleasure in virtuous actions. Doing good things grudgingly or under compulsion doesn't make you good. So perhaps our aesthetic responses—the way we react to things emotionally according to our ideas of beauty—can be an index of moral character, to the extent that they correlate our actions with our pleasures. For instance, if someone does something of which we disapprove, our tendency to also disapprove of the doer will be tempered if we believe that the action pained that person. Conversely, we will more readily hate the sinner along with the sin if we believe the sinner took pleasure in the sinful act. The statement, "This hurts me more than it hurts you" is an attempt to deflect moral culpability by linking the speaker's actions to pain rather than pleasure for the speaker.

Three and a half centuries after Aristotle, Jesus implied a similar thing in his Sermon on the Mount. Over against his hearer's received wisdom about righteous behavior, he set a far more stringent requirement of an inwardly righteous disposition.

You have heard that it was said to the people long ago, 'Do not murder, and anyone who murders will be subject to judgment.' But I tell you that anyone who is angry with his brother will be subject to judgment...You have heard that it was said, 'Do not commit adultery.' But I tell you that anyone who looks at a woman lustfully has already committed adultery with her in his heart...You have heard that it was said, 'Love your neighbor and hate your enemy.' But I tell you: Love your enemies and pray for those who persecute you, that you may be children of your Father in heaven. (Matthew 5, *passim.* NLT)

Notice that Jesus doesn't say the Law is wrong—simply that it isn't enough, that a deeper conversion is required that goes beyond conventional moral codes. The Law is black-and-white; conversion of the heart involves many hues.

The Greeks set "noble and beautiful," against "ugly and base," more than they did "right" against "wrong." (The ancient Hebrews were similarly preoccupied with "honor" vs. "shame.") One can argue that moral decision-making has more to do with concrete aesthetic responses to certain courses of action than with abstractions about "right" and "wrong." We do or refrain from doing, not because deeds are "right" or "wrong," but because they are attractive or repellant.

Consider the well-known story from the Gospel of John:

The scribes and the Pharisees brought a woman caught in adultery, and having set her in the center of the court, said to (Jesus,) "Teacher, this woman has been caught in adultery, in the very act. Now in the Law Moses commanded us to stone such women; what then do you say?" They were saying this, testing Him, so that they might have grounds for accusing Him...(Jesus) said to them, "He who is without sin among you, let him be the first to throw a stone at her."... When they heard it, they began to go out one by one, beginning with the eldest, and He was left alone, and the woman, where she was, in the center of the court...Jesus said to her, "Woman, where are they? Did no one condemn you?" She said, "No one, Lord." And Jesus said, "I do not condemn you, either. Go. From now on sin no more." (John 8:3-11, NASB)

I have heard this passage read ever since I can remember, but I cannot recall ever having heard a sermon mention what to me is a very salient point: *the eldest present were the first to leave.* The Law made the woman's adultery and her death-by-stoning morally equivalent, and Jesus did not contradict the Law. Nevertheless the accusers, convicted by Jesus' words, were unable to fulfill the Law's requirements. Why? I submit that, through the lens of their own sinfulness, they saw that although stoning the woman was *right* in the eyes of the Law, at the hands of the sinful self-righteous it would be an *ugly* act—and the mature onlookers, because of their longer experience of struggling humanity, were the first to realize it.

There is a kind of moral rigidity that is the province of youth. The less experience one has of the slings and arrows, the easier it is to see the world in primary colors; a sense of moral nuance, like an eye for tints and shades, takes time and experience to develop. As Aristotle warned in his *Ethics*,

...the young man is not a fit student of Moral Philosophy, for he has no experience in the actions of life, while all that is said presupposes and is concerned with these: and in the next place, since he is apt to follow the impulses of his passions, he will hear as though he heard not, and to no profit, the end in view being practice and not mere knowledge.

This is the reason, I believe, that the mature are often patronizing at best and dismissive at worst toward the moral certainties of the young. Yes, some of us grown-ups have become cynical, and some are too invested in the status quo to be supportive of the reforming zeal of youth. Many of us are just tired. But most of us also have as keen a sense of justice as in our youth—but, like old warriors, we know better how to apply ourselves. My old dog doesn't bother to bark at the mailman any more, but the puppy barks at everybody. The dog is as zealous for our safety as the pup—he just knows what's worth getting excited about and what isn't.

I cringe when I hear how the young and zealous talk about "those people" who, in their ignorance and ill-will, stand in the way of the perfect world they would otherwise have built by now. They may or may not be right, but their contempt is ignoble and their thoughts ugly—as mine have often been. Excess of certainty is an especially poisonous excess.

Aristotle defined virtue as the mean between excess and deficiency. One isn't good because one has a surfeit of some virtuous quality, but because one knows how to walk the thin line between too little of it and too much. Locating that tipping point and maintaining the balance is an aesthetic process, a skill-set one acquires over time, like knowing when to stop adding paint to a picture, notes to a score, words to a story or pepper to a broth. It would take very little exaggeration of the most desirable features in a beautiful face to render the face ugly. The secret of beauty is knowing when enough is enough.

The onlookers who walked away had had enough, and Jesus awakened their aesthetic sense to find the balance between deficiency and excess of justice. In my own moral strivings I have been trying to cultivate the same outlook. It is easy to talk oneself into believing that what one does is just, but it is harder to snow oneself about what is beautiful. I may think it right to scream at a representative during a town hall meeting, but can I really regard it as noble? It may seem right to do unto others as they have done unto us, but can any amount of blather make it seem honorable? I can talk myself into the right forever, but when I try to talk myself into the beautiful, repentance comes.

"When I was a child," wrote Paul, "I talked like a child, I thought like a child, I reasoned like a child. When I became a man, I put childish ways behind me." (1 Corinthians 13:11) In America today, we too often mock nuance, on-the-other-hand indecisiveness, and the willingness to change, and we reward those who scorn repentance as weakness. I believe this is because, although we are actually looking for the noble and beautiful, we tell ourselves that we are looking for the right. If we were to know ourselves better and consciously pursue balance, harmony and proportion, we might drop the stones and grow into moral adults.

But if it is relatively easy to see how maturity would broaden one's moral and emotional palate, it may be less obvious how depression could do so. After all, if my life before things fell apart was slathered in the hot sauce of a very limited range of emotions, the life of depression is bogged down in rumination, emotional inertia, and an oppressive grayness. My old pasted-up life was generally angry, while my new fallen-apart life is often testy. Neither offers much of a range of options.

But the difference is that while my old self was morally rigid because of the stories I told myself about "right" and "wrong," and emotionally crippled by the disconnect between my ambitions and my life as lived, depression—while it exchanged up-front pain for background malaise—forced me to give those obsessions a rest, at least from time to time. Simple sadness gave me a breather from fiery anger; subtle regret offered a respite from bitter frustration; complicated moral equivocation gave relief from simple, and toxic, self-righteousness. Looking back, it seems as though my emotional intensity was eating me up from the inside, and depression called a much-needed time-out. "We can view depression not as a mental illness, but on a deeper level, as a profound (and very misunderstood) state of deep rest, entered into when we are completely exhausted by the weight of our own (false) story of ourselves." (Foster)

And the undifferentiated leaden oppressive grayness of depression does not last forever. And when it withdraws into remission, it leaves behind a heightened emotional sensitivity, a broader range of feeling tones, as yogurt or sherbet cleanse the palate of fiery peppers that keep one from tasting anything else. This is the treasure of darkness—a whole world of feelings to which we had been previously unavailable, and a range of moral possibilities of which our prior certitude had made us insensible. I am more labile now than I was before, more in touch with my actual (as opposed to habitual) feelings; more able to take quiet delight in small things; more fully present to people, events and blessings that would once have failed to hold my attention; less ready to judge and condemn. Life is no longer passing me by while my attention is elsewhere, and it is more, if more subtly, flavorful than it was.

[viii] A portion of this essay first appeared at ProgressiveChristianity.org under the title, "Drop the Stone" on February 11, 2010. Used here by permission.

Chapter 9

Mining for Outrage

Cognitive psychology has become aware that much depression is maintained, even generated, by getting caught up in negative patterns of thinking. –Martin Laird, *Into the Silent Land*

A dog returns to its vomit. –2 Peter 2:22

* * *

The narrator of John Irving's *A Prayer for Owen Meany* is an American expatriate living in Toronto in the late 1980's. During the Reagan administration's Iran-Contra scandal—the President's cronies were caught illegally selling arms to Iran to fund their covert war against the democratically elected government of Nicaragua—the expat, John Wheelwright, finds himself unable to resist buying and reading *The New York Times*. Even though he knows the news from home will make him furious, even though his students know they can avoid work by "getting him going" about American current events, he keeps returning to The Gray Lady for his daily dose of anguish. "I simply must stop buying *The New York Times!*" he tells himself—but he keeps buying it.

What torture Wheelwright could have wrought for himself in the Internet Age.

In 2015, I don't have to leave my house to find things to fuel my rage. I can sit at my desk for hours, clicking on links to articles, blog posts and comments that I know ahead of time will likely incense me; that is, in fact, precisely why I click on them. Sometimes it feels like I'm on a search-and-destroy mission, ruling out innocuous-looking items and zeroing in on the toxic ones—except, of course, that the only one being destroyed is me.

I call this behavior pattern "mining for outrage." One can mine the newspaper, the Internet, or even one's own memories for things to make oneself miserable. Claudia Weaver, whom Andrew Solomon interviewed in *The Noonday Demon: An Atlas of Depression,* perfectly described the internal/mental version of MFO:

I have a lot of trouble remembering positive things when I'm depressed. I go over and over the negative things that people did to me, for which I have an elephant's memory, and times when I was wronged or shamed or embarrassed, and they escalate and become worse than they were in real life, I'm sure. And once I think of one of those things, I can think of ten and that leads to twenty more. (Solomon 136)

Boy, did that sound familiar. I have spent hours upon hours sniffing out painful memories like a tracking hound, my mind dwelling on recollections of things my parents did to me, things my teachers did to me, things my girlfriends did to me, things the church did to me, grants I didn't get, performances I didn't get, awards I didn't get, jobs I didn't get. As soon as I've either exhausted one topic, or reminded myself that I'm not making the best use of my mind and I should probably chill out, I find that I've moved on to another topic more or less before I know it.

I find that being emotionally "stuck" and caught in a repetitive mental loop go hand in hand; the two conditions feed on one another. When I can't pull myself out of a bad mood, it is my negative thought patterns that get in the way, and when I try to change my self-absorbed thought patterns, my toxic mood lands me back in them before long.

Psychologists call this particular type of psychologically inflexible behavior *rumination,* and the attendant mood state *emotional inertia.* Although we generally think of emotional stability as characteristic of psychological well-being, it is actually a fine-tuned emotional responsivity, continually adjusting to changing internal and external circumstances, that characterizes mental health. It is this flexibility of mood, this "capacity for dynamically responding to fluctuating situational demands," that is lacking in depression. (Koval, Kuppens and Allen) So if our emotions cannot adapt to changing stimuli, we go looking for stimuli that will justify and feed our intractable emotions.

Political blog comments are rich ground for outrage mining. In my case, the right wing bigots, gay-baiters, Muslim-haters, and other assorted trolls are not the problem. I hold no illusions about being able to change these peoples' opinions, though I do believe there is value in humanizing their enemy in myself. The longer I gently question their positions without taking their bait, the harder it is for them to maintain a monolithic view of their opposition—or so I tell myself. Their abuse and non-responses don't bother me much.

What keeps me awake at night is when people with whom I believe myself to be on the same side are abusive to me—especially when they seem determined to judge my insides by the Religious Right's outsides. Fundamentalist Atheists—with whom, as a non-dualist, I actually have a lot in common—are a good example. (By "Fundamentalist Atheist" I mean atheists who, like fundamentalists of all kinds, confuse religion with science. The salient difference is that while religious fundamentalism posits a false dichotomy and declares for religion, atheist fundamentalism posits the same false dichotomy and declares for science.) No matter how gently I try to explain to them that I don't believe in what they mean by "God," either, all I get in return is scorn and contempt from people too self-righteous to view the religious landscape with any nuance, or to make any distinctions between religious fundamentalists and religious progressives. And that is when my outrage-mining pays off too richly, going beyond feeding my bad mood to force-feeding it, tipping the scales from depressive inertia to raw pain and useless anger.

"I don't even get agitated when people tell me they don't believe in God at all," wrote Eknath Easwaran. "Usually they are thinking of something, or someone, external, some extraterrestrial being swinging between Neptune and Pluto. When I use the word God, I am not referring to anything separate from us, but to the divine ground of existence of which we are all part." (Easwaran 20)

But I never even get far enough with aggressive atheists to propose that their "God" may be a straw man, and that they and I doubtless share more than they think. This is a shame, because I could easily make common cause with them in several areas. But I no longer try, because it is just too bootless and painful.

I recently had the following exchange in the comments section of a blog entry on a gay-rights website:

Angry Gay Pagan Dude: (not his actual user name—and I only deduce that he is a pagan from pictures I saw on his Instagram stream)—Typical lying Christian scum. (This was in response to something one of the anti-equality commenters posted.)

Me: That's pretty hateful language, [Angry Gay Pagan Dude.] I am a Christian, and I support marriage equality. Please don't be a bigot.

AGPD: Go drink bleach, Christian scum.

Me: 1) Bleach is harmless, AGPD; it will not hurt you if you drink it. 2) Why do you insist on talking like the bigots? LGBTQ+-friendly Christians are legion—we just don't grab headlines like the haters do. Don't act like them.

AGPD: Speak all you want, I would never trust you.

Me: So this isn't actually a discussion, is it? It's just a pissing contest. That's really sad. Good thing all the weddings done at my church are valid whether you "trust" me or not.

AGPD: You would be a "righteous" christian who would stand first in line to throw gay people into Hitler's ovens. I have known your hate filled christian kind all my life.

(I need to pause here to apologize to Anna Sarkeesian, Felicia Day, Laci Green, and all the other courageous feminists who have braved the wrath of the testosterarchy online. While I have always sympathized both with their cause and their methods, I confess to having been skeptical about the reportedly traumatizing effects of hateful Internet comments. Considering how lacerating I found this one salvo from this one irrational troll, I am now prepared to believe without question the claims of feminists about being forced to change jobs and/or addresses in response to torrents of violent online hate speech. My duty to you all.)

This stung, inasmuch as the AGPD didn't, in fact,

"know" me from Adam's off ox.

Me: It is painfully obvious that you don't know the first thing about me or my "kind." What are you even basing this on? Can you read minds? Have you seen my other comments on this thread? Upon what possible evidence do you dismiss me as "hate filled"?

Predictably, no answer was forthcoming; people like this are in it for a dust-up, not a dialogue. When faced with a non-combatant response, they clam up—generally from an inability to maintain their position effectively but, I suspect, also out of pure passive-aggressive meanness in this case. I believe this angry, probably disturbed man—who had likely suffered all manner of indignity and abuse at the hands of bigoted yahoos who call themselves Christians—could see that I was hurt by his hateful words and subsequent silence.

Unfortunately, being shut out behind a wall of indifference is my own personal Room 101—the "Ministry of Love's" torture chamber in George Orwell's *1984* in which the torture regimen is custom tailored to the individual victim. ("You asked me once, what was in Room 101. I told you that you knew the answer already. Everyone knows it. The thing that is in Room 101 is the worst thing in the world.") I began obsessively checking for a response, and when none came, I tried again.

My church began celebrating same-sex weddings almost the moment it became legal in our state—and before that, we were blessing gay unions. I am not your enemy, and neither is my church—nor a possibly-surprising number of other churches like it. Do you have so many allies that you can afford to spit on some?

Obviously, I was losing my cool. The AGPD's bilious words ate at me; they are eating at me as I write this. I simply cannot stand it that someone would judge me wrongly and then not hear me out. Maybe I didn't get enough emotional mirroring in my pre-verbal years, who knows?

After discussing this with my therapist, I decided the time had come to curtail my MFO as much as possible. It is bad enough when it simply maintains emotional inertia; when it goes beyond that into stoking low-level fury, it has gone from serving no good purpose to being actively harmful.

I've stopped listening to right-wing talk radio, deleted my Disqus account, and am trying to stay alert for signs of internal outrage-mining. Because it has become obvious to me that I am like one of those glasses of water in the old plastic wrap commercials—the ones in which they'd seal the glass with wrap and turn it upside down to show how strong the seal was. I can seem, even to myself and even when life is turning me upside down, fully self-contained and functional. But if anything—even so small a thing as a hateful comment from a total stranger—should puncture the thin layer that's holding the sadness in, it will spill out all over the place and soak everything.

Chapter 10

The Waters of Babylon

It is hopelessness even more than pain that crushes the soul. –William Styron, *Darkness Visible: A Memoir of Madness*

* * *

Psalm 137 is one of the best-loved and most-quoted psalms—up to the point at which it becomes horrifying. Written by a Jew who had been taken captive, along with many others, into Babylon after Nebuchadnezzar conquered Judah, it is the lament of an exile—someone ripped away from plans, hopes, dreams, ambitions, religious life, home and happiness.

By the waters of Babylon we sat down and wept,
 when we remembered you, O Zion.
As for our harps, we hung them up
 on the trees in the midst of that land.
For those who led us away captive asked for a song,
and our oppressors called for mirth:
 "Sing us one of the songs of Zion."
How shall we sing the Lord's song
 upon an alien soil?
If I forget you, O Jerusalem,
 Let my right hand forget its skill.
Let my tongue cleave to the roof of my mouth if I do not remember you,
 If I do not set Jerusalem above my highest joy...
O Daughter of Babylon, doomed to destruction,

Happy the one who pays you back for what you have done to us!
Happy shall he be who takes your little ones,
And dashes them against the rock!

The poem's violent ending places it amongst a group of psalms known as the "curse psalms," or "imprecatory psalms". These are often an embarrassment to the faithful, who are anxious to show in their religion a source of peace, and a fund of ammunition for the enemies of faith, who are anxious to find anything but.

These psalms were even in the news briefly when certain Christian demagogues with theocratic tendencies began urging their followers to pray them against President Obama—in particular Psalm 109:8: "May his days be few, and may another take his office."

I think it will be useful to examine this psalm using the medieval "threefold exegesis," in which a passage is understood in 1.) its literal sense, 2.) its allegorical sense, and 3.) its moral sense. By the time we're done, I think this psalm will seem much less incomprehensible—particularly as it relates to depression.

1. The Literal Sense

The Literal Sense asks of the text, "What happened? What do the words say?"

In 586 BCE, the southern kingdom of Judah was defeated, and its capital Jerusalem destroyed, by the forces of the Babylonian Empire. Lamenting by the Tigris and Euphrates Rivers, the exiles hung up their harps on the overhanging trees rather than satisfy their captors' demands for some Jewish songs. In addition to not wishing to gratify their tormentors with a performance of their music that their hearts would plainly not be in anyway, they also believed that, though there was only one God, "maker of heaven and earth," that God lived in a special way in Israel and, in particular, upon Mount Zion, where the Temple had been. It just wouldn't have seemed right to sing the songs of Zion outside of the "promised land."

Mingled with the exiles' grief was the knowledge that the prophet Jeremiah had been warning them for years about the conquest, and instead of listening to him and mending their ways, they had thrown the prophet into a cistern and, after eventually pulling him out, imprisoned him in the guardhouse. (Jeremiah 38:6-13) In that sense, they had brought their misfortune upon themselves.

2. The Allegorical Sense

In confronting these psalms, many thinkers have chosen to treat them as spiritual allegories—as C.S. Lewis does in *Reflections on the Psalms*. By interpreting them as referring to the things of the soul, Lewis says,

> *...I can even use the horrible passage in 137 about dashing the Babylonian babies against the stones. I know things in the inner world which are like babies; infantile beginnings of small indulgences, small resentments, which may one day become dypsomania or settled hatred, but which woo us and wheedle us with special pleadings and seem so tiny, that in resisting them we feel we are being cruel to animals...Against all such pretty infants...the advice of the Psalm is best. Knock the little bastards' brains out. And "blessed" he who can, for it's easier said than done.* (Lewis 136)

While this approach may well have worked for Lewis, it strikes me as what my Pennsylvania Dutch grandmother would have called "going round Robin Hood's barn"—meaning traveling a needlessly circuitous route. The psalms are neither theology, nor law, nor history, nor eschatology; the psalms are *prayer*. As such, it seems to me that they are the most human part of the whole Bible—the record of a people who told it like it is to God, without holding back or gussying up. They are direct, and I think our interpretation of them ought also to be direct. Accordingly, my own allegorical response to this psalm is much more raw than Lewis's.

I had a preliminary glimpse of the utter hopelessness that grips the Psalmist during the winter after my first bout of graduate school. With the ink well-dried on my M.Mus sheepskin, and having looked in vain for a job in, or at least adjacent to, my field without success, I was working at a federal government ore depot—a stockpile of "strategic natural commodities" hoarded during the Cold War but no longer useful. I was alternately shoveling gravel into bins and sorting out clumps of clay and dirt from gravel on a conveyor belt. At -10°F, the hopper froze up and the supervisor hoisted me up in the bucket of an excavator so I could jump up and down on the frozen gravel.

I remember eating lunch alone in my car, in panic despair that I was living then the life I would always live— that my training, talent and hard work were never going to amount to anything, my abilities never be put to use and my acquirements abandoned like so many piles of superfluous cryolite. Had there been a river there, I'd have wept by it, an exile from my true home. Had I read Dickens' *David Copperfield* at that point, I would have known down to the ground the blight that the ten-year-old protagonist felt upon beginning work in Murdstone and Grinby's warehouse:

No words can express the secret agony of my soul as I...felt my hopes of growing up to be a learned and distinguished man, crushed in my bosom. The deep remembrance of the sense I had, of being utterly without hope now; of the shame I felt in my position; of the misery it was to my young heart to believe that day by day what I had learned, and thought, and delighted in, and raised my fancy and my emulation up by, would pass away from me, little by little, never to be brought back any more; cannot be written.

But it was at the end of my second quarter-century that I felt something like the full horror that drove the Psalmist to infanticidal fantasies. After a morning—one of a seemingly interminable series—of struggling in vain to accomplish something grade homework, write a blog entry, compose music, research, apply for chaplain jobs, change the smoke alarm batteries, *something*—I found myself curled up on the couch in a fetal position, a black hole of self-loathing and frustration. Remembering my wife's and therapist's oft-repeated advice to be self-compassionate, I decided to take a break and do something that would make me happy for a while before returning to work.

I could not think of a single thing.

Nothing I used to do for pleasure—take care of the garden, take the dogs to the park, read a novel, visit the arboretum or my favorite coffee house, sit on the front porch and play the concertina—these things, which had given me joy for many years, didn't even come into my mind, or if they did, they kept to the shadows where they couldn't be clearly seen.

Sure that I would never be happy again, that my depression was permanent, that everything that gave me solace was lost to me forever, I panicked. It was the only time I had ever thought of suicide. Certain that nothing would ever be better, that I was not going to get well, I found the idea of going on living terrifying. I was a permanent exile from my own resources. At that moment, if I'd been sure that what had happened to me had been done to me by someone else—if I'd had as clear an enemy as the Psalmist had—I don't know what I wouldn't have been capable of wishing or doing.

I suppose my approach is more mythical than allegorical, strictly speaking, in the sense that, in allegory, there is a specific one-to-one correlation between elements in the story and the corresponding elements in life-outside-the-story; for instance, when we see populists and union leaders becoming indistinguishable from the bourgeoisie, we know what a great allegory George Orwell's *Animal Farm* was. Lewis's infantile-thoughts-to-Babylonian babies correspondence is allegorical.

A myth, on the other hand, does its work in a much less pat way; it is more of an analogy-by-*Gestalt* than a fully-worked-out scheme in which this-stands-for-that. But perhaps for that very reason, the great myths continue to live themselves out in our individual lives.

Anyone who's ever tried to run a household—especially one that includes kids—knows what it is to live the myth of Sisyphus, the king of Thessaly who was condemned for eternity to roll a boulder up a hill only to watch it roll down again every time. The floor is no sooner mopped than it is dirty again, and dinner is never *made*, once and for all; which of us has never had an inkling of how Sisyphus must feel?

And Tantalus! Every time a piece of my music is short-listed without being chosen for performance, I remember you; every time I think I've got the drop on life in the morning only to be discouraged again by dinner time, I feel your pain. Patron and spirit-familiar of everyone who's ever had the prospect of advancement, promotion or success dangled "tantalizingly" before them only to have it snatched away over and over again—all who wanted to marry but never did, who tried and tried at life but never succeeded, who went again and again to call-backs and second interviews without being cast or hired, all the Willy Lomans and Eleanor Rigbys and Broadway Danny Roses who snatched defeat from the jaws of victory—all of us stand with you in Tartarus, up to our necks in water that recedes when we bend to drink, while the tempting fruit that hangs over our heads withdraws beyond our grasp when we reach out for it. Your anguish lives in all of us.

If there is a directly allegorical element in my response to Psalm 137, it is probably The Crab Bucket. No crab ever escapes from a bucket, because the other crabs will pull the escapee back in.

Whenever I make any of what I consider spiritual progress—or even when I simply have several good days in a row—the bad feelings and negative thoughts will come rushing in, dragging me back in the Slough of Despond like so many crabs re-bucketing a confrere. Spend a few days being mindful, happy and in-the-moment, and the other crabs in the bucket will take notice. (This dynamic, I suppose, is the same thing as what my evangelical colleagues would describe as a "demonic counter-attack.") These crab-thoughts that take captive my better self just as it begins to breathe the air of freedom and ease are begging to be dashed against some rocks, in my estimation.

"There is, Father of Love, an agony at the heart which is fighting against that calm resignation which Thou teachest," wrote Swami Vivekananda. It is our personal crab-bucket, our individual Babylon.

3. The Moral Sense

Lewis wasn't using Medieval Three-Part Exegesis in his treatment of Psalm 137 (though I have no doubt he was well aware of it and could have used it if he'd chosen). Nevertheless, I think Lewis was using the moral lens when he saw that, "in the Psalmist's tendency to chew over and over the cud of some injury, to dwell in a kind of self-torture on every circumstance that aggravates it, most of us can recognize something we have met in ourselves." (Lewis 23) (See the section on "rumination" in *Mining for Outrage*, above.)

I recognize something of myself in Psalm 137; in fact, I'm pretty sure I know exactly when the horrible baby-dashing idea occurred to the Psalmist. At the moment the anonymous exile fully realized that he was *never going back* to Judah, that his humiliation and defeat were really permanent, that his hopes were well and truly dashed and there was absolutely no remedy this side of the grave, "the terror of the pain never ending" (Strauss 125) came upon him, and he wished a bloody death upon his tormentors' children. I can see it all.

Psalm 137 challenges us to see the big picture behind what looks like irrational hatred and violence—to strive to see even terrorists, suicide bombers, and their more "legitimate" counterparts in the standing armies of their more-powerful enemies, in a put-yourself-in-their-shoes way. As the nineteenth century English Baptist and famed interpreter Charles H. Spurgeon wrote about the final verse of the psalm,

Let those find fault with it who have never seen their temple burned, their city ruined, their wives ravished, and after children slain; they might not, perhaps, be quite so velvet mouthed if they had suffered after this fashion. It is one thing to talk of the bitter feeling which moved captive Israelites in Babylon, and quite another thing to be captives ourselves under a savage and remorseless power, which knew not how to show mercy, but delighted in barbarities to the defenceless. (Spurgeon)

"Without a vision," says the proverb, "the people perish." (Proverbs 29:18) It may be that after so many years of hatred and conflict, the vision of peace and freedom has been lost or obscured, and people hurt because they have been hurt, without any idea, in the absence of a redemptive vision, how or why to do otherwise. If people seem crazy, it may be because they have forgotten how not to be. To quote Claudia Weaver again:

What really matters to me? I'd ask myself. I don't know. What would make me happy? I don't know. Well, what do I want? I just don't know. And that totally freaked me out. (Solomon 136)

-Chapter 11

Participant Observer

Shame seems to drive my psychic engine. I don't know why this is so. All I know is that I am excessively calculating, especially when I appear not to be, in order to avoid being shamed. –Dennis Covington, *Salvation on Sand Mountain: Snake Handling and Redemption in Southern Appalachia*

* * *

I was commissioned to teach a few English Country Dances at a parish Christmas party. We hired musicians; I arranged the music and rehearsed it with them. People told me for weeks that it "sounded like fun," and they were "looking forward to it." The big night came.

No one would dance.

Years later, remembering how foolish I felt standing alone in the middle of the floor while people clustered by the walls staring at their feet, I am still angry.

I'm angry about the way people don't sing in church, and the nonsense they mumble about "not knowing the hymns" and being "intimidated" by the choir.

I am angry because I once canvassed for a tenant advocacy group in a poor neighborhood, and no local businesses would advertise in our newsletter, *Tenant Action,* because it had the word "action" in the name.

People are mealy-mouthed cowards, and I can't stand them.

Of course, I find freestyle dancing, with no predetermined steps, intimidating. But that's different.

And the very thought of karaoke terrifies me. But that's different, too.

A friend keeps inviting me to the Philadelphia LGBT Hindu Satsang, and I'm worried that all the men will be fitter and better-dressed than me. But really, there's no comparison, right?

Right.

The fact is, I am brutally impatient with people who are intimidated by things. Except the things I'm intimidated by. Because we condemn in others what we reject in ourselves.[10]

I've done things that people have called "brave": blogged about my depression, attended worship services of other faiths, visited prisons, sung right out loud in front of God and everybody. But outside of my narrow comfort zone, I am so eaten up with self-consciousness I can barely function. I am so terrified of being shamed that I have installed a sort of security system through which I monitor every door and hallway for potential threats. It's exhausting.

In his book *The Wee Free Men*, Terry Pratchett introduces Tiffany Aching, a nine-year-old girl destined to become a witch. Despite her tender years, she has developed two of the indispensable aptitudes of witchcraft: First Sight and Second Thoughts.

First Sight means that you can see what really is there, and Second Thoughts mean thinking about what you are thinking. And in Tiffany's case, there were sometimes Third Thoughts and Fourth Thoughts, although these were quite difficult to manage and sometimes led her to walk into doors. (Pratchett 155)

---

[10] I don't know who originally said this.

At the beginning of Tiffany's witching career, the Kelda, or matriarch, of a clan of faerie folk called the Nac Mac Feegle, tells her something else about herself—that she will always be set apart, watching life without being able to join in with abandon; always self-conscious, like an anthropologist participant-observer in her own life.

'Tis the First Sight and Second Thoughts ye have, and 'tis a wee gift an' a big curse to ye. You see and hear what others canna', the world opens up its secrets to ye, but ye 're always like the person at the party with the wee drink in the corner who cannae join in. There's a little bitty bit inside ye that willnae melt and flow. (Pratchett 158)

The first time I read that, I had to pause to catch my breath. The Kelda was describing me! The person who has never once in his life danced as though no one were watching, who never throws himself recklessly into the fun, the person "in the corner who cannae join in"—that's me, I thought! There's a little bitty bit—maybe a good-sized bit— inside me that willnae melt and flow. I just have too much running internal commentary preventing my loosening up, and too great a fear of appearing ridiculous to let myself go.

I haven't heard anyone else talk about this crippling self-consciousness as a component of depression, and maybe it's a peculiar artifact of my own experience. But I have heard from many sources that social isolation is both a contributor to, and a result of, being depressed—and I know from experience that self-consciousness exacerbates social isolation.

Psychologist Philippe Rochat, in his book *Others in Mind: The Social Origins of Self-Consciousness,* posits that the very thing we call the "self", to the extent that such a thing can be said to exist, is formed in the interaction of the mind with the outside world. Guilt, shame, embarrassment, self-consciousness, preoccupation with reputation—all these, Rochat maintains, are the result of our having evolved with the ability, unique among species, to perceive ourselves as the objects of other peoples' thoughts. We come to see and understand ourselves through other peoples' evaluations of us, and our selves are formed by the fear of others' rejection.

As someone who spent his brainy and overweight childhood being pretty relentlessly bullied, I get this. Years and years of jeering and ridicule led to the installation of that internal monitor that is ever watchful for potential openings for rejection. And though people who have experienced more than their share of rejection may have a proportionally outsized self-consciousness, I think most of us have such an internal monitor to one degree or another.

For instance, actors talk about "the Watcher"—a part of oneself that sits on the shoulder and comments on the performance while it is still in progress. And while one generally wants to shrink one's Watcher as much as possible (it cannot be gotten rid of entirely) in order to enter fully and unselfconsciously into the role in performance, most actors I know will admit that they make use of it in regular life. During any situation in which new emotions are being felt, or familiar ones felt to a new degree or in a new way, the Watcher will say, "Remember this; you can use it later." I read an interview with Paul Reiser in which he said his wife could tell, in the midst of an argument, when he was taking mental notes for things he could use in future episodes of *Mad About You*.

As a writer, I understand this; I, too, have what Stephen Sondheim called "a part of you always standing by."[11] If I could just send it away when I wanted to, I'd be all set.

I mentioned my impatience with timid people. I'm also pretty hateful toward ignorant people. As a brainy kid, I was always being made to feel like a freak for knowing things other people didn't. Being able to say, "I'm not weird for knowing—you're stupid for not knowing" was a self-preservation strategy. But it isn't useful in an adult who wants to live a godly and compassionate life. Self-consciousness, defensiveness, fear of rejection and of looking foolish—they become, over time, an emotional straitjacket, and it becomes harder to take the risks necessary if you want to reach out to, and help, others. If you get laughed at enough for being yourself, you learn, as the song says, to "Conceal, don't feel."[12]

I suppose this explains why, having heard my children playing the score from *Frozen* innumerable times, I went to see the movie by myself while my family was out of town. I was absolutely captivated by the song "Let it Go"— an anthem to self expression and integrity toward one's inner truth. It made me think of all the time my childhood self spent hiding, shrinking back, fearful of discovery. In my more self-conscious moments, I imagine I must have looked a little creepy—a middle-aged man sitting by himself at a kids' movie with his shapeless old-guy hat pulled down over his face to hide his tears. But in my better moments, I couldn't care less.

---

[11] Sondheim, Stephen. "Finishing a Hat," from *Sunday in the Park with George*

[12] Lopez, Robert, Anderson-Lopez, Kristen. "Let it Go," from *Frozen*

-Chapter 12-

Sins of the Fathers[ix]

"...the wrong that rouses our angry passions finds only a medium in us; it passes through us like a vibration, and we inflict what we have suffered." –George Eliot, *Scenes of Clerical Life*

* * *

I try, I really do. I always make an effort to be civil online. Of course I fall short occasionally, but I always try. Then I read this in my Facebook feed:

In Best Buy and there's a HORRIBLE child! Mother keeps saying "Shush! No you can't have it." All the while he's screaming, crying and carrying on "I want this!" He has to be about 6. If it was my kid, a good spanking on the butt with a "There! Now you have a reason to cry!"

I was appalled at the number of people whose comments expressed regret that a good old-fashioned spanking is now considered abuse by a politically correct world. I knew how the prophet felt when he wrote, "there is in my heart as it were a burning fire shut up in my bones, and I am weary with holding it in, and I cannot." (Jeremiah 20:9) I simply had to weigh in on this.

Now, I started off slowly, by responding (relatively) positively to the few dissenting comments that were posted.

Well said, Dxxxx. Everyone—teachers, other parents, (etc.)—tell me how well-behaved my children are, and we have *never* hit them, nor *would we ever. Hitting a child is barbaric.*

Amen to that, Fxxxx. I remember many a beating from childhood, but not a single "lesson" I supposedly "learned" from them. Hitting a child is for people with no self-control who have run out of ideas.

It was at about this time that the originator of the thread admonished me to "be respectful of others." To which I replied:

I call them like I see them, including calling bullshit when I hear it. Hitting children is barbaric, period. If that makes me "disrespectful," so be it.

Which is pretty harsh, for me.

I walked around for several days with a ball of fury roiling in my stomach as I obsessed over this thread. And then, by some cosmic coincidence, the Beit Shemesh school story broke in the news.

You may have heard of the Haredim—the ultra-Orthodox Israeli Jewish sect that clashed with police over what they see as the forced secularization of their close-knit religious neighborhoods. The town of Beit Shemesh was the epicenter of the unrest. On January 4, 2012, a 19-year-old woman soldier was harassed—called a "slut" and a "shiksa"—for refusing to move to the back of the bus with the other women. (Though not legally binding, many people observe this *mehadrin,* or strictly kosher, custom on bus lines that pass through Haredi neighborhoods.)

The tensions came to a head over a religious school built on the unofficial borderline of Beit Shemesh's Haredi enclave. A group of the black-hatted ultra-Orthodox men lined the sidewalk outside the school to spit on, shove and scream at the children, whom they called "whores" and "Nazis" because they found their dress—conservative by most standards—"immodest." Eight-year-old Naama Margolese became a *cause célébre* when her story, in which she described the "tummy ache" she endured each day out of fear of the protesters—appeared in news outlets around the world.

Looking at the rage in the faces of these men at the presence of bare-armed second-graders, it would be easy to dismiss them as one-dimensional, bigoted zealots. And I certainly deplore their tactics, which include spitting and screaming at children, destroying "objectionable" merchandise in stores, and pepper-spraying girls who walk down the street in the company of boys. Though I am sympathetic to their ultimate aim of living a godly life, I find their apparent vision of that life repellant.

Of course, to these Haredim, not only the rightness of their beliefs, but the appropriateness of their responses is axiomatic:

"I think sometimes they're not sensitive to the impact of what they're saying because to them, the fact that a woman and a man should not sit together on the bus, it's so obvious." (Hersh)

(This, I believe, is why so many social conservatives resent exposure to the news media. The whole "liberal media" canard aside, I think they believe at some level that outsiders—who cannot even see how obvious it is that women and men should not sit together in public, for example—simply cannot possibly understand, and are therefore unfit to judge, their actions.)

Tactics aside, even the content of their belief system is strange to me; what possible harm could there really be in a t-shirted second-grader? The belief that these children are corrupting the morals of the community is as odd to me as the belief that gay marriage will somehow undermine straight marriage.

But here's my confession: though I do not agree with what they believe, and do not condone what they do, *I understand how they feel.*

Let me explain.

My children, like all children, have a repertoire of behaviors that really push my buttons. (Note: teachers, neighbors, Sunday School leaders, other kids' parents, relatives, even total strangers—everybody tells us that our kids are exemplary. This is *my* problem, not theirs.) My older daughter in particular has been making exploratory forays into disrespectful teenage behavior that I find it incredibly difficult to deal with because if I had acted like that, *I'd have gotten hit.* And while I have, thank God, broken the family cycle of physical violence, when my daughter treats me in a way that would have gotten me belted or slapped, I have no tools to use, no inner flowchart to consult, because events in my own childhood simply never flowed past that point.

My parents instilled in me what I, borrowing from Kant, call a "categorical imperative": *children must never defy, or otherwise show disrespect to, parents. Period.* And while I have rejected my parents' ways of enforcing this rule, I evidently internalized the rule itself at a deep level.

A violation of a categorical imperative is *something that cannot be,* something absolutely intolerable—like anti-matter which, if left alone, will blow up the universe. It simply must be done away with at any cost. And while both the specific beliefs and the enforcement strategies differ wildly between the Haredim spitting on other peoples' children and me shouting at my own, I am sure that the emotional content is drawn from the same well. When the irresistible force meets the immoveable object, there is going to be hell to pay.

I've been told—and I'm prepared to believe it—that these aggressive Haredim are an atypical minority within their community. And while I haven't any idea whether the extremists routinely beat their children, I don't believe the Haredim are merely being stubborn or willfully stupid when they defend their actions—they simply haven't the mental categories to accommodate any other interpretation of the world or support any other behavioral strategies. The categorical imperative builds a wall imagination cannot penetrate nor thought see beyond.

Most often, we pass along to our children the very same categorical imperatives that marred our own childhoods: think of Celie in Alice Walker's *The Color Purple*, advising Harpo to beat his wife Sophia as her own husband beat her, because she had internalized the message that wives must obey their husbands.

Think of parents who bully or reject their children because no son or daughter of theirs is going to be a faggot. Think of Afshan Azad, who played Padma Patil in the *Harry Potter* movies. Her brother beat her and incited her father to attempt to kill her because she was dating a Hindu. To them, it simply *could not be* that their sister and daughter would "dishonor" them in that way. And yes, this belief that a man's honor is dependent upon the behavior of his female relations, and that women who sully it must be dealt with through brutal punishments up to and including "honor killings," strikes me as nothing more than playground preening writ large and deadly, the cant of backward savages.

But reject as I may the content of their beliefs and

their methods for enforcing them, I cannot deny that, in some fundamental way, I know how they feel. I, too, have had it literally beaten into to me that some things simply cannot happen and must not be allowed to exist. I am lucky in that my present social milieu does not support corporal punishment; if it did, I might have visited the sins of my fathers upon my children as much as anyone else. I probably wouldn't—I'd like to think I wouldn't—but I couldn't swear to it.

I know I sometimes exasperate people by my unwillingness to sit in judgment even on people whose behavior I find repellant. And yes, I do have my own lines in the sand—obviously, child-beating is one. But who knows what, had I been born into other circumstances, I might myself be capable of? And how can I even begin to understand people as radically different from me as the Haredim—or even people who practice or condone corporal punishment—unless my gaze is "lit up" by love, and a willingness to enter into others' feelings and the causes of them?

...surely, surely the only true knowledge of our fellow-man is that which enables us to feel with him—which gives us a fine ear for the heart-pulses that are beating under the mere clothes of circumstance and opinion. Our subtlest analysis of schools and sects must miss the essential truth, unless it be lit up by the love that sees in all forms of human thought and work, the life and death struggles of separate human beings.[13]

---

[13] George Eliot, *Scenes from Clerical Life*

[ix] "Sins of the Fathers" first appeared in *Elephant Journal* on January 16, 2012, in slightly different form. Used here by permission.

Chapter 13

I am Going to Die^x

It is funny how mortals always picture us as putting things into their minds: in reality our best work is done by keeping things out.
—C.S. Lewis, *The Screwtape Letters*

* * *

A few years ago I had what now appears to have been a migraine aura—a strange visual disturbance that made it seem as though someone had smeared living, squirming Vaseline all around the periphery of my visual field, while shimmering zig-zag lines floated into and out of view. I also felt a little dizzy and shaky. And while none of these symptoms may seem particularly alarming, I had never had a migraine before (that I knew of) and didn't know what an aura looked like—neither did I know that they are more common in men than in women, or that they tend to occur "later in life."

Now, in spite of carrying some extra weight, I am in pretty good health. But when a doctor who happened to be nearby began asking me questions about funny smells or tastes, numbness and tingling—questions that made it clear that he suspected a stroke—I began to panic a little, becoming so pale and alarming that my friends called my wife to leave work and take me home.

Of course, I felt ridiculous on the surface—I was, after all, just fine—but deeper down I knew I had something very important to learn from the incident:

I am not reconciled to the inevitability of old age, sickness and death.

I heard the singer Bhagavan Das tell a Buddhist story about a sea turtle in the depths of the ocean who comes up and, as if by chance, puts its head through a small wooden ring floating on the surface. The probability of this happening, he said, is the same as the probability of a human birth. So a human birth is an immeasurably precious thing, and there are both a staggering opportunity and an immense responsibility bound up with this earthly life. Consider Jesus' famous Parable of the Talents. (A "talent" was an amount of money measured by weight, according to whatever precious metal was being measured.) Jesus compared the Kingdom of Heaven to a man about to depart on a long journey, who entrusted his wealth to three trusted servants, in differing amounts according to the abilities of each.

After a long time the master of those servants returned and settled accounts with them. The man who had received the five talents (said)... 'Master, you entrusted me with five talents. See, I have gained five more.' His master replied, 'Well done, good and faithful servant! You have been faithful with a few things; I will put you in charge of many things. Come and share your master's happiness!'

The man with the two talents also came. 'Master,' he said, 'you entrusted me with two talents; see, I have gained two more.' His master replied, 'Well done, good and faithful servant! You have been faithful with a few things; I will put you in charge of many things. Come and share your master's happiness!'

Then the man who had received the one talent came. 'Master,' he said, '... I was afraid and went out and hid your talent in the ground. See, here is what belongs to you.'

His master replied, 'You wicked, lazy servant!...Take the

talent from him and give it to the one who has the ten talents. For
everyone who has will be given more, and he will have an abundance.
Whoever does not have, even what he has will be taken from him.
(Matthew 25:14-29[14], NIV)

The servants' situation is the one in which we all
find ourselves. When we come to give an account of our
lives, what return will we be able to make on the talents
with which we have been invested?

I took my children to a maple sugaring festival along
with a friend of theirs from school. Run by the city, the
festival is an impoverished affair without any music, so as I
often do I brought along my concertina. As I sat on a
bench and played some traditional American tunes, a few
curious children and their parents stopped to listen. Off to
one side, I heard a mom drawing her little girl's attention to
what I was doing. "Look at that, honey—do you know
what that is?" she asked.

"An old man?" the little girl replied.

(Breathe…breathe…)

Now, any normal forty-five-year-old person might
think this funny, in a cute, Art Linkletter sort of way. But it
bothered me. A lot. And it still does. When I heard the
words "old man," the one that came to mind was the one
Walt Whitman wrote of, "who has lived without purpose,
and feels it with bitterness worse than gall."

I have two fantastic children and a wonderful wife
who puts up with my *mishegoss;* I am still making music and
doing my best to alleviate the suffering of my fellow
creatures. But in spite of everything I have always thought I
believed, I still struggle to find peace with the fact that I am

---

[14] Edited for length

probably more than halfway through my life without anything to show that I am, in any worldly sense, a "success." I haven't set the world on fire! I haven't "made a difference!" If I were George Bailey, I'd have gone to jail!

Insufferable, I know. And yes, I am mentally ill. But I don't believe I am alone in this. Isn't our whole culture frantic to keep us distracted? There are now video screens at the gas pump. We can watch movies on our phones. News has degenerated into entertainment, while entertainment has been elevated to news. We as a society are, as sociologist Neil Postman put it, "amusing ourselves to death." What are we as a people trying so desperately not to face?

Yes, we don't want to think about death. And there are a lot of frightening things afoot these days that are hard to face, from climate change to resistant disease germs. Our children will inherit an unstable world from us after we die, which will not be very long from now.

But I think there is more to it than that. I believe that not only do we not want to think about death—we don't want to think about life, either. We have a high calling, we humans. When my children try to sneak away from the table without drinking their milk, I remind them that a farmer and a cow worked hard to make that milk, and it won't do to waste it. Well, the universe has labored to make us, and yet we let ourselves go to waste. Though we don't like to think about it, "we know that the whole creation has been groaning as in the pains of childbirth right up to the present time." (Romans 8:22) And in order not to face the charge we have to keep, we allow the world to direct our attention here, there, everywhere but the present moment—which is, as it turns, precisely where the treasure is. Now is the day of salvation.

In the midst of life, we are in death, the *Book of Common Prayer* tells us. Our lives are precious, and they are finite. Work while you have the light.

---

[x] "I Am Going To Die" first appeared in *Elephant Journal* on February 16, 2011, in a slightly different form. Used here by permission.

Chapter 14

Dream of the Red Dog

It's springtime, and I'm in the basement of
The house where I grew up. I'm with my Dad.
We're doing spring things—getting ready for
The growing season. There's a hanging wire
Basket that I want to take upstairs
To store the long-awaited fruits.
                                        But then
My Dad stops, turns his head, and sniffs the air,
Alarmed, and says, "There's a red hound nearby."

I lumber up the stairs, and at the top—
Somehow it's not the old house, but the next,
The one my mother died in—I look out
The kitchen door that leads to the garage.
A menacing red dog, coyote-like,
Looks back, and grins, and springs. I slam the door
And hear the brute bounce off, and shoot the bolt.
That thing wants in. I hear it growling still.

How did my father know, from way down there,
I wondered, what was stalking us outside?
But then I thought about it, and I knew.
He had quintuple bypass just last year;
He knows the pong of that red dog, all right.

* * *

-Chapter 15-

Rope Trick[xi]

To the ego, the present moment is, at best, only useful as a means to an end. It gets you to some future moment that is considered more important, even though the future never comes except as the present moment and is therefore never more than a thought in your head. In other words, you are never fully here because you are always busy trying to get elsewhere. —Eckhart Tolle, *A New Earth: Awakening to Your Life's Purpose*

That which is above is as that which is below, and that which is below is as that which is above. —The Emerald Tablet of Hermes

* * *

I used to smoke weed when I was younger, until I discovered that the world is fascinating already. When I let the dogs out at night and hear the wind soughing in the neighbor's gigantic sycamore tree, its looming form blotting out the stars over our back yard, it is fascinating; when we open up the Styrofoam cooler in the shed and find that the children have filled it with grass while playing Underground Railroad (apparently the grass represented provisions of some kind) it is fascinating; when I am bawling out my five-year-old, and my six-year-old tells her, "Daddy's not saying you're not a good person, Sophie," it is altogether fascinating.

Of course, we all need fascination——what Paul Gauguin called "a sense of the beyond, of a heart that beats." One evening while our first daughter Clare was still a baby, my wife and I were having dinner at a friend's house when Clare began to get fussy. Our hostess picked her up and took her across the room to look at a candle. "Let's get fascinated!" she said. Our baby stared, rapt and slack-jawed, at the flickering flame, and I saw for the hundredth time how numinous and mesmerizing the world was in her infant eyes. Not presuming to have all the answers about anything she saw, or to be able to control things by naming them, she was happy to let the world be its fascinating self—almost as though she could detect "the dearest freshness deep down things"[15] with some special sixth baby-sense. "We see the world with the five senses," said Swami Vivekananda, "but if we had another sense, we would see in it something more." (Vivekananda, *Jnana Yoga* 28)

Longing for this "something more" is, I believe, the reason people smoke weed; having lost the baby-sense, people turn to THC to open their minds to the bottomless fascination of the world. Because we no longer have eyes to see and ears to hear, we have lost touch with the infinite, absolute, eternal life that animates our narrow, relative and temporary lives. "I tell you the truth," Jesus said, "unless you change and become like little children, you will never enter the kingdom of heaven." (Matthew 18:3) But changing is hard, and chemicals can seem to bypass the need for it. It's not for nothing that the body's neurotransmitter that the cannabinoids in marijuana mimic is called "anandamide"; *ananda* is Sanskrit for "bliss." We will, apparently, take our bliss any way we can get it.

People do drugs because they want, as Marianne Williamson put it, "a different experience of what is." And it seems to work because "what is" is slippery and unstable;

---

[15] Gerard Manley Hopkins, "God's Grandeur"

so much so, in fact, that many things can alter your roadmap of reality. My first year or so of temp work was strictly blue-collar, from assembly line and warehouse work to flagging traffic to dumping buckets of frozen aloe vera onto a conveyor belt. During a run of success as a composer, when my temp agency supervisors noticed my name appearing in the local papers and heard me interviewed on public radio a few times, I started getting "cleaner" jobs, like moving lawyers' offices and setting up insecticide displays in supermarkets—jobs for which I wore a tie. I was astonished at how differently people treated me—even out in the country where nearly all the men wore work boots and lined flannel shirts—when I wore a white shirt and a tie. I was the same person who had worn the reflective orange vest the week before, but when the complexion of the *maya,* or illusion, around you changes, people perceive and respond to you differently. If a drug could make that kind of difference in our experience of the world, you couldn't keep it on the shelves.

(Sometimes a little *maya* bait-and-switch can be fun. During a period when I was getting a lot of commissions and performances as a composer, expensively-dressed people would approach me at post-concert receptions and ask me where I taught. "Actually, I work at K & W Tire," I'd tell them. The visible discomfort in their faces and bodies before they extricated themselves from my company and went to freshen their drinks was priceless.)

So what happens when our experience of our lives is wildly out of tune with any rational assessment of our circumstances? During a rehearsal at another musician's house, my hostess handed me a drink. Distracted with a piece of sheet music, I took the glass, seeing peripherally the clear liquid inside and assuming that it was water. I took a drink and was appalled by the nastiness of the fluid in my mouth—which, as it turns out, was Sprite. I like Sprite. But because I had been expecting water, and my mind was configured for it, I nearly choked on the Sprite.

My life is like that. I have a fantastic life: two wonderful, intelligent, thoughtful, exuberant children, a loving wife who puts up with me and keeps me honest and earns enough to allow me to stay home, keep house and garden running, be there when the kids get home, compose and perform music and do freelance ministry. But because it isn't what I was expecting, I often experience my life as confining, unfulfilling. I expected it to be full of height and depth and *gravitas,* and have found it full of dog fur and goutweed. I looked forward to being intellectually and aesthetically stimulated on a daily basis. (What I thought would happen about the dog fur and goutweed I don't know.) I thought I would feel more important.

There are no Desert Fathers around when you need one to adjust your attitude. I am haunted by the story of the young monk who went to Abba Moses for advice on spiritual advancement. "Go and sit in your cell," the Abba told him, "and your cell will teach you everything." Your life as it is, here and now, is gravid with everything you need to know—but it seldom appears that way. And yet, if we had eyes to see—if we could get our thoughts out of the way of our perceptions, if we could stop labeling everything with a "yes, I know all about that"—who knows what we could detect in the seemingly undifferentiated landscape of our lives? If we had no mental category for "green," the woods would be a riot of color.

As a child I watched a lot of TV. And of course, life on TV always seems more interesting and fulfilling than life elsewhere, as it's meant to. My own life involved a lot of being bullied on the schoolbus and playground, so TV had a lot of allure for me. Moreover, my budding religious sensibility was stewed in a sort of vindicationalism: I got picked on at school, but I was going to reign with the saints in the Kingdom. So there were some pretty powerful incentives to regard day-to-day life as unreal—a preparation for some more fulfilling, fascinating "real life" that was going to happen at some time in the future.

The worst of this is that so much good passes us by while we are on the lookout for something better. I read somewhere that most of us meet some 1400 people during our lives with whom we could be compatible life partners. So why aren't we all happily married? Because we see other people through the filter of the ridiculous ideas in our heads.

And not just people. Early on in my folksinging days, a number of friends urged me to "go on the circuit" as a folk musician. I was reasonably good at it, and I loved doing it. But something had happened in my brain that made me regard ballads, pub songs and fiddle tunes as mere avocation, and somehow frivolous; my *real* work, I always told myself, was in the musical world in which I was being trained in graduate school. It didn't matter that playing my concertina and inviting my listeners to sing along made me happy; I was a *composer*—which is to say, a "serious" musician. I cringe with shame to recall this—some of the most phenomenal musicians I have known have worked in traditional music—but that is honestly how I thought about it. (Note: I know I've talked about this subject before; it looms large over my life.)

I could watch a group of novice dancers and extend a tune until they had completed a figure before moving to the next part of the tune, I could invent lyrics on the spot, I could improvise a musical accompaniment to a *Commedia dell' Arte* performance, I had several hundred songs in my head ready to go at any time—but those skills all involved music in the service of something else, while *serious* music existed purely as a sonic object to be politely contemplated in a concert or recital hall. So I spent years of my life, great pots of money, untold hours of unflagging industry and enough emotional energy to power a small city trying to fit into that world and make that music. Why didn't I see earlier that I was slashing my way through the wrong jungle?

Half my lifetime ago I had an experience that, had I known at the time how to interpret it, could have saved me a lot of anguish and wasted time. But life, as Kierkegaard pointed out, can only be understood backwards, and it would be many years before the lesson the experience had to teach me would finally become clear.

The summer after I graduated from college I was with a group of friends, and we had all eaten psilocybin mushrooms. For some time, I didn't understand what the fuss was all about; I didn't seem to be what I thought of as "tripping" at all. "I just feel stoned," I said to a friend. "That's it," she replied: "Just relax into it."

And she was right: as soon as I let go of my prefabricated mental construct of "tripping" and simply allowed my experience to be what it was, I discovered that I was indeed tripping, and in a big way. It was all happening already, but my willing-it-to-be had kept it from my awareness. Sober, I had the life I wanted already, and I didn't know it, because I *never* "relaxed into it." The Zen teacher Shunryu Suzuki made a very similar point about the pursuit of *satori*, or sudden awakening, in meditation:

(A)s long as you think, "I am doing this," or "I have to do this," or

"I must attain something special," you are actually not doing anything. When you give up, when you no longer want something, or when you do. not try to do anything special, then you do something. When there is no gaining idea in what you do, then you do something. (Suzuki 28)

Relax into it.

Now, let me be clear: I am not recommending mind-altering drugs. There are far too many uncontrolled variables, too many dangers. And the mind, moreover, is like a computer: garbage in, garbage out. The second time I used mushrooms, I was in a worse state of mind than I realized—my always-incipient depression was closer to the surface—and the drug released an amazing trove of mental garbage. The experience was so terrifying that I vowed never to do it again, a vow I have kept for over a quarter century.

Finally, drugs and the like only seem to be expanding our minds while we are under their influence; they make no real and lasting change in us. Eckhart Tolle posited that, while things like meditation can take us above our thoughts, things like drugs and television take us below them; both can free us from our thoughts, but not in equally beneficial ways. (Tolle 230)

Sri Ramakrishna, the nineteenth century Bengali saint whom many Hindus regard as an Incarnation of God, used a telling metaphor about wisdom seekers "doing something" in their quest for God. They climb the stairs of renunciation one by one, Ramakrishna said, and when they finally reach the roof, they discover that it is made of the same brick and lime as the stairs. (M) We are not going anywhere, because we are already there—or at very least, "there" is not essentially different from "here," no matter how much we sacrifice to our belief that is surely must be.

What is here is also there; what is there, is also here. Who sees multiplicity but not the one indivisible Self must wander on and on from death to death. (Katha Upanishad II.i.9)

I'm tired of wandering; if the "one indivisible Self" resides in us all, where is there to go? The Infinite does not "go" anywhere. It is—you are—already there.

Jesus was apparently trying to get his hearers to "relax into it" when He told them, "The kingdom of God does not come with your careful observation, nor will people say, 'Here it is,' or 'There it is,' because the kingdom of God is within you." (Luke 17:20b-21) There is no place to go; it is already here—you are already there.

This is how the world regains its fascination: by our looking at it neither through the eyes of deluded desire that compare it to something "better" in our heads, nor through the eyes of calculation and greed for gain, but through the eyes of the Kingdom within, the eyes of a little child who sees that see the world afresh and full of possibility. Not of drugged sleep, but of alert wakefulness.

"Could you not stay awake with me for one hour?" Jesus asked His disciples on the last night of His earthly life. (Matthew 26:40) I think He asks each of us the same thing—"Keep awake, for you know neither the day nor the hour." (Matthew 25:13) When Jesus asks us to keep awake with Him, he is inviting us to share in His divine life and ministry. According to poet Andrew Hudgins, Jesus is

...someone walking through his life—or hers—
Until God whispers, It's you. And God's ignored...
Or does God simply choose us all? (Hudgins)

So OK, smartass, I tell myself: if you're Jesus—if

you abide in Him and He in you like vine and branch (John 15:15)—stay awake with yourself! Don't be continually falling back into the sleep of life inside your head, don't be always drawing a veil of expectations and desires between yourself and the circumstances in which God and your *karma* have placed you. Don't end up like Jacob, who had to physically wrestle with his Creator and sustain a painful injury before he could say, *"Surely the Lord is in this place, and I did not know it."* (Genesis 28:16b)

Shankaracharya, the father of non-dualist Vedanta philosophy, used the image of coiled rope in a dimly-lit room to explain our cognitive dysfunction. If upon entering the room we mistake the rope for a snake, we will be unable to see the rope, and we cannot see the rope until we stop seeing the snake. As long as we see our lives as preparatory, stalled, unreal or unfulfilling, we cannot see them as numinous, fascinating, *"charged with the grandeur of God."* These, says Paul Simon's song, are the days of miracle and wonder—but *all* days are the days of miracle and wonder if we are fully present to them. The earliest Christian texts speak, not of the "return" of the Christ, but of Christ's "revelation;" when the scales fall from our eyes, we will see that we are already in God. This is surely what the Psalmist longed for when he prayed,

When I awake, I will be fully satisfied, for I will see you face to face. (Psalm 17:15b, NLT)

---

xi "Rope Trick" first appeared in *Elephant Journal* under the title, "Why People Smoke Weed" on November 17, 2010, in a slightly different form. Used here by permission.

-Chapter 16-

What's In You For Me?[xii]

Contrary to popular understanding, contemplation does not imply quietness or withdrawal. Instead, it is a quality of immediate, open presence that is directly involved with life-as-it-is. –Gerald May, *The Awakened Heart: Opening Yourself to the Love You Need*

What I say to you, I say to all: keep awake. –Jesus (Mark 13:37)

* * *

In *A Hitchhiker's Guide to the Galaxy,* Douglas Adams introduced us to the Someone Else's Problem (S.E.P.) Field, a cloaking device that allows things to go unnoticed—such as a gigantic alien spaceship hovering over a cricket match—by tapping into peoples' natural predilection not to see things they are unprepared to accept.

I have discovered that I project a number of such fields onto other people, making actual human beings invisible behind the veil of my ideas about them. As a public service—in case we ever meet in person—here is a partial list of the fields I may project onto you:

The P.O.F. (Pokey Old Fart) Field. If you stand still in the middle of the supermarket with your cart blocking the aisle, or drive a car ten or more miles per hour below the posted speed limit, all I am likely to notice about you is your advanced age and how damned slow and in-the-way you are. You may have risked your life in the Invasion of Normandy or fed transients during the Depression, but that isn't getting me where I want to go right now.

The U.S.C. (Un-Spiritual Christian) Field. Sure, I see you showing up for church, volunteering to do stuff—but it's obvious that you haven't cultivated a deep relationship with God through spiritual practice like I have. You must be really shallow.

The S.Y.P. (Spiritual Yogi Poser) Field. Your cloud of woo-woo swirls around you like so much Patchouli incense; why should I try to look past it into your obviously deeply flaky soul?

The C.J.W. (Canvassing Jehovah's Witness) Field. I simply cannot see a person under the overwrought suit—only a polite but inarticulate Watchtower dispenser. Bring it, bitch; I know more Bible than you.

The S.I.J. (Self-Important Jackass) Field. I don't actually lose much sleep over this one (though maybe I should.)

And finally--and perhaps most pernicious:

The H.C. (Hot Chick) Field. This one, along with its near relation, The M.I.L.F. Field, is particularly difficult because, besides being highly opaque, obscuring the person around whom I project it almost entirely, its influence often outlasts the interaction, in the form of what classical Christian language calls "impure thoughts." So while you—a complex, multi-dimensional human being—are kind enough to be talking to me, I am only listening to a stereotype, while under the almost complete control of my inner fifteen-year-old.

Christian moral teaching condemns such unchaste thinking irrespective of whether it leads to illicit behavior, because of the inherently objectifying effect it has on the way we perceive our fellow children of God. Fortunately, we are liable, not for every thought that pops into our heads, but only for the ones we willfully cultivate.

The familiar measure of the sinfulness of such thoughts was of course whether they had been intentionally "entertained," or merely noticed and released...Truth be told, I was often a willing and cordial host, coaxing these thoughts to stay for dinner and dessert, and perhaps even to spend the night if this were not an inconvenience. (Mahan 26)

So I have bad news and good news. The bad news is that if you find yourself projecting a field around someone, it is highly ineffective (for me, anyway) to tell yourself to stop. "Don't objectify that Hot Chick in the short shorts," I may tell myself—or "his reflexes aren't what they used to be; he's only trying to be safe"—or "all that arrogance is probably meant to shield a very frightened and insecure psyche"—but I will still be fighting an uphill battle trying to see through the field to the person behind it.

The good news is that spiritual practice works. This is easy for me, a Christian Yogi, to forget, because of the emphasis that both Yoga and Christianity place on mystical experience. As long as I have yet to be "caught up into the third heaven" (2 Corinthians 12:2) like Paul, or engulfed in samadhi like Ramakrisha, it's easy to feel like my daily sadhana isn't "working." But my soul knows it is, however slowly, because of "the love, joy and peace it receives bit by bit from God as it grows." (Underhill 66)

Do not be conformed to this world, but be transformed by the renewing of your mind, so that you may prove what the will of God is, that which is good and acceptable and perfect. (Romans 12:2, ESV)

The Greek word Paul uses for "transformation" is *metamorphosis*—to "change beyond" where we started out. Another New Testament word for renewing of the mind is *metanoia*. Usually translated as "repentance", it is better understood as a radical change of mind and heart, occasioned by an experience of clarity and profound understanding.

I fear that some of Christianity has emphasized the dramatic metanoia over the quotidian metamorphosis, with the result that people look for something profound while missing the personal growth they are actually experiencing. If we really have to prove we are "born again" by speaking in tongues, then God help those of us who simply aren't constituted that way. This is why the Zen teacher Shunryu Suzuki hardly ever talked about *satori*—sudden enlightenment experience—at all: he didn't want people to fixate on dramatic mystical events and become discouraged if they were delayed in coming. (Suzuki ix)

Of course, even if we never experience dramatic, life-changing events, it is still incumbent upon us to change.

Truly I tell you, unless you change and become like little children, you will never enter the kingdom of heaven. (Matthew 18:3, NIV)

I have found that no amount of willing myself to change really has any effect—not internally, anyway. I can "fake it till I make it" sometimes, behaving as I know I ought to until the behavior carves a new set of samskaras in my chitta (literally "mind-stuff"), and of course going around the sun a certain number of times imparts some experiential wisdom, but for the most part, any positive changes that have happened in me have their roots in regular sadhana, or spiritual practice, both formal and informal, on the cushion and off.

One of these is my increasing ability to release thoughts instead of being hijacked by them. I am still far from the "freedom of Christ" (Galatians 5:1) or the *moksha* (liberation) of the advanced yogi, but as I learn to check in with myself, letting go of thoughts and awakening, however briefly, from my field-projecting dreams into the wakefulness of the present moment, my "increasing availability to the truth" (May) is giving me the knack of "seeing through exterior things, and seeing God in them." (Merton) This is a skill I have developed on the cushion, and which I am now able to deploy in day-to-day life. "What we plant in the soil of contemplation, we reap in the harvest of action."[16] I've noticed that the New Testament epistles—especially the letters of Peter—refer far less to the "second coming" of Jesus than to His *apocalypsis*, or "revelation." (Literally, "taking away the veil.") To my mind, this implies that we will see Jesus when the scales fall from our eyes; if we are, as the baptismal vow charges us, to "seek and serve Christ in all persons,"[17] He must be here already, waiting to be revealed. Christ must be here right now, behind the fields we project around other people, eager to be sought and served.

The name for this non-objectifying approach to other people is called *chastity* in the classical language of the church. Now, we tend to think of chastity as having to do with sex. (This is because we tend to think of everything as

---

[16] Meister Echhardt, a 14th century German mystic
[17] Baptismal vows, *Book of Common Prayer*

having to do with sex.) A fuller discussion of sexual chastity, continence and celibacy is out of place here, and has been done elsewhere. I am more interested in chastity in the broader sense, as set forth in the Principles of the Third Order of St. Francis:

Our chief object is to reflect that openness to all which was characteristic of Jesus. This can only be achieved in a spirit of chastity, which sees others as belonging to God and not as a means of self-fulfillment.

By this definition, chastity is that quality of mind whereby we are able to perceive others, not in relation to ourselves and our agendas, but as complete in themselves.

You've probably seen at least one old cartoon in which two characters, marooned on a desert island or adrift in a lifeboat, each seem to see the other transformed into a steak or a turkey leg or something. Then they start shaking salt on each other and whetting their carving knives. That's what unchastity does to us: transforms other people before our eyes from something actual into something potential—with the potentiality being wholly in relation to ourselves.

Capitalism is rife with unchastity. Before I had CDs to sell, I had audiences; now I have potential CD buyers. So not only is the quality of my relationship to my listeners less immediate than it was, but I cannot be fully satisfied with the *inter*action unless it ends in a *trans*action. I used to want to connect with people; now I want to profit by them.

How often have I been at a gathering and mentally divided everyone into those who could help me, and those who couldn't? Does a person's personal magnetism increase with their potential to buy what I'm selling, get me gigs, advance my career or introduce me to other useful people?

Unchastity doesn't always appear in such gross forms—there are subtle forms, too. Will a person's conversation amuse me? Or instruct me? Or provide material I can steal to use on the next person? How will this person respond to me? Will they be impressed by my knowledge and accomplishments, feeding my sense of self-worth? Will they find me interesting and funny, thereby helping me find myself interesting and funny?

In his "Essay Concerning Technology," Martin Heidegger describes people's tendency to view things not as things, but as potential other things. Our gaze transforms a river into a potential power source, a forest into potential building materials. Nothing is simply what it is—everything is "standing in reserve," as Heidegger puts it.

More than any other single thing, I have found that this tendency to objectify everything and everyone, to place everything and everyone in reserve, to see the present moment only as an opportunity for getting what we think we need to insulate us from what may happen in the future, to place a lens of calculation and evaluation between ourselves and the world, so that we never actually inhabit the here and now among the who and what of our lives—this is, for me at least, the single greatest fuel source for depression. When everyone and everything exist only as potential, there can be no real joy here and now. When the mind is forever spinning around a dreaded future or a regretted past, longing for a thing not yet possessed or an outcome not yet attained; when the mind is so transfixed by the birds in the bush that it is blind to the bird in the hand, no amount of blessing in this place and this moment can penetrate our defenses and point us toward happiness.

What frightened creatures we are, always worried

that the future will bring scarcity and lack unless we grab all we can in the present, always hopeful that every person we meet and every situation in which we find ourselves can be turned to our advantage. This must be why Jesus told his disciples not to worry about what they were to eat, drink or wear: so that our human interactions would be untainted by the dirty devices born of our fear.

One unexpected payoff of an extended sabbatical from the "working world" is that I no longer spend my days willing other people to do things so that I can be happy. Ambition transforms everyone we come in contact with into "relevant" or "irrelevant" to our desires. How can I manipulate circumstances so as to get this person to do what I want? Not wanting anything in particular from anybody makes one more chaste.

This was one of the best things about being a Eucharistic Visitor—someone who takes Communion to parishioners who cannot attend church. Most of them are elderly, confined either to their own homes or to a retirement home, and I was more free of personal agenda in my interactions with them than in almost any other interactions. Through that work, I began learning to really pay attention to people.

All the Gospels give accounts of Jesus seeming to read people's minds; Ramakrishna, also, was said to be able to "see right through a man." (M) I don't think there was anything supernatural involved in those incidents. If Jesus "didn't need to be told about people, for he knew what was in a person," (John 2:25) I think it was because he was paying attention. He was able to size people up as they were, because he wasn't trying to size them up as potential means for his own self-fulfillment. Instead of things standing-in-reserve for use, He saw people, complete and precious in themselves.

When we are spiritually chaste, seeing our fellow children of God as ends rather than means, not calculating how we can profit by them, we can be more present to them as they are, and more responsive to their needs. When we no longer cast perceptual fields around our fellow creatures, we may see them as God sees them—not as somebody else's problem, but as our own.

---

xii "What's In You for Me" first appeared in *Elephant Journal* on July 17, 2010, in a much shorter form. Used here by permission.

-Chapter 17-

Beautifully Falling Apart

My house is full of books I can't read and records to which I can't listen and photos at which I can't look because they are too strongly associated with the past. —Andrew Solomon, *The Noonday Demon: An Atlas of Depression*

Don't you ever think of things that make you shiver?...Little bits of things make me do it;—perhaps a word that I said and ought not to have said ten years ago;—the most ordinary little mistakes, even my own past thoughts to myself about the merest trifles. They are always making me shiver. —Anthony Trollope, *Can You Forgive Her?*

* * *

I have a recurring dream scenario in which I am trapped in a dark, cluttered, dirty basement, trying to escape and make my way upstairs. (Once the basement was full of water, like some primordial chaos.) In one iteration of this theme, I actually managed to get upstairs, climb up on a bookcase, push open a trapdoor in the ceiling, and squeeze my way through a narrow opening into a clean, spacious, empty attic, brilliantly lit from a gable window.

Using the common interpretation of a house as symbolic of the self, I imagine this dream signifies my being trapped among the detritus of my "lower self" and striving to reach the peace and light of my fully-realized, "higher" self. And what's amazing is that I ever get out of the basement at all, because *I never throw anything away.*

Shame from childhood. Embarrassing things I said

or did as a teenager. Anger at things done to me before some of my younger friends were born. None of it ever goes away; it all just floats and ferments in my personal Slough of Despond. I have no doubt that the junk in my dream basement—and the bright emptiness of the dream attic—refer to these clinging afflictive thoughts, and to their blessed eventual absence.

At least once a day during bad times, I find myself frantically evincing an absorbing interest in some trivial activity or some object in the room, or wildly casting around for something to focus my attention on other than the embarrassing memory that has come to the fore in my head. On the worst days, I can spend hours wandering from one remembered slight or personal outrage to another. I always find them exactly where I left them; there is, apparently, no curb pick-up for them.

When someone from my past appears in my Facebook friend requests, I have a deer-frozen-in-the-headlights moment during which I try to work out whether this is someone I need to be hiding from. Even if I have no bad memories associated with that person, I fear later contact from some mutual connection from whom I imagine I may need to conceal myself. I can never put as much distance as I want between the apprehensive new me and the embarrassing old one.

Another recurring dream motif I have is the journey-in-stages. In this set of dreams, I am leaving one train and frantically searching for my connecting train for the next stage of the trip; sometimes I am making a bike-to-train connection, or setting out on my bike over mountains or on four-lane highways. Sometimes I am on my way to an urgent appointment; other times I am trying to get home. But in all cases I am leaving my first conveyance and setting out on, or trying to find, my connecting transportation, and time is always running out.

I suspect this dream is trying to tell me to move on, get to the next stage—find that clean, spacious, well-lit place before I am too old to enjoy it, before the wind passes over me and I am no more. The old conveyances have gotten me as far as they can; the new ones are waiting for me—but they won't be waiting forever.

Sometimes it isn't the painful memories of the past, but the stark contrast between some imagined glory days and the allegedly lackluster present that makes me shrink from my recollections. It is too painful to be reminded of how happy I supposedly was in the good old days.

So often I have revisited old haunts, trying in vain to recapture the feelings I had when I was first in those places years ago. Not only could I not feel as I had in the past, I couldn't enjoy the places in the present. In his first memoir, Kirk Douglas described going back to Paris after the war and finding it not as exciting as when he was stationed there. He eventually realized that he was actually seeking his twenty-two-year-old self—who was, of course, not there to be found. Like him, it took me lots of puzzled standing around and staring to figure this out.

"Why are you standing there looking up at the sky?" the angel asked the apostles after Jesus' ascension. I wonder how the Apostles felt about the places they had been with Jesus after Jesus was gone? Did they see the streets of Jerusalem as they appeared when they walked them with their teacher, or as they actually were in the present? How long did they see through disciples' eyes before their Apostles' eyes finally opened?

They had left behind their old lives, let everything go to pieces, in order to follow Him, and from that windy hill outside Jerusalem, the days that were past, as full of hardship as they had undoubtedly been, must have looked warm and inviting. How they must have longed to return to the relative simplicity of those days when following Jesus just meant literally following Him down the road.

But those days had to give way in order for the new thing God was doing to take shape. The old conveyance that had gotten them that far was at the end of the line, and they had a connection to make. And if everything old hadn't gone to pieces, nothing new could be built. Things have to fall apart, and there's no going back, no matter how messed up they may seem in these latter days.

There's a wonderful 15th-century English Christmas lyric that briefly alludes to the traditional explanation of how things got so bad—Adam and Eve eating that fruit— then moves on to something positively startling: if the apple had never been taken, Mary would never have become "hevene Queene." Without falling on earth, in other words, humanity could never be exalted in heaven. "Blessed be the time," the poet exults, "That appil taken was!"

These people had an average life expectancy of 35, more of their children died than survived, they wore their hats at the table to keep the lice out of their food, and yet they praised God for the Fall of Man. *Blessed be the time that apple taken was.* As though Eden had been some kind of infantile Pleasantville. And who wants to live in Pleasantville, anyway—the fictitious 50's sitcom into which two 90's teenagers are mysteriously transported in the movie of the same name? In Pleasantville—"a place where life is simple, people are perfect, and everything is black and white"—people do not suffer, but they cannot really live or love. Love is too messy a thing for a black-and-white world, and the suffering, sympathetic God is a stranger wherever falling apart is unknown—no matter how good the put-together past may look from the present vantage point. Because the attic may seem empty, we forget how cluttered and dirty the basement was. Blessed be the time.

As my friend, the singer-songwriter Abigail Palmer, put it:

> *I remember well the days*
> *When I existed in warm haze*
> *We lost ourselves from the start*
> *We beautifully fell apart*[xiii]

[xiii] Abigail Palmer, "Shedding Shadows." Used by permission.

PART II

The Road to Real

-Chapter 18-

Make Our Lives a Blessing

(God) gives his sunlight to both the evil and the good, and he sends rain on the just and the unjust alike. —Matthew 5:45

* * *

    This section of the book is not about depression *per se,* but about the broader issue of suffering. Many great minds have engaged this topic for as long as great minds have done anything, I suppose, and I do not pretend to exhaust the possibilities of the subject to any but my own satisfaction.

    One hears a lot of unfortunate and glib assessments of human suffering, from "everything happens for a reason" to "shit happens." All, it seems to me, are flawed, and none are really helpful. This section is my small attempt to remedy both deficiencies. My concerns in this area are more pastoral than purely philosophical; I want to understand suffering mainly for the sake of making it bearable.

    During my stint of Clinical Pastoral Education in hospice ministry, I visited a large, apparently robust, healthy-looking man who was dying of cancer. He was alert, oriented and sitting up in bed. After some small talk, we began to talk about his condition and trajectory. Finally, he seemed to reach a decision and, with a puzzled look he asked, "How will I know when I begin to die?"

    After taking a moment to recover from the bombshell of a question, I replied that I couldn't, of course, tell him what it felt like on the inside, but I could tell him what it looked like from the outside.[18] As people draw closer to death, I told him, their attention often turns inward; they may be aware of the presence of others, and hear and understand what they say—in fact, they often show strong evidence that they are doing so—but their focus is more on their interior life than on exterior events. As I explained this, he nodded with a thoughtful expression on his face.

When I visited him a week later, I found he had suffered a precipitous decline, and lay grey-faced and obtunded on his pillows. I spoke with his wife and sister for a while, and in the course of the conversation told her about the talk I'd had with her husband. Lighting up, she said, "Oh, that was you! He said that conversation really helped him." This is my goal in seeking understanding: to make suffering more comprehensible to the extent necessary for making it more sufferable.

This man's wife and sister were typical of a lot of patients' family members I saw—well-turned-out, immaculately dressed, elegantly coiffed, urbane, articulate and self-possessed. Until I led us in prayer. Prayer brings things below the clavicles like nothing else; within seconds, self-possession gave way to healing tears. This happened as regularly with working-class families as professional, Jewish as well as Christian, lax as well as devout. Prayer goes to the heart of things. "Out of the fullness of the heart the mouth speaks," Jesus said (Luke 6:45); stand still a moment and let the well fill up, and the living water will flow.

---

[18] In doing so, I was greatly helped by having read Maggie Callahan and Patricia Kelley's book, *Final Gifts: Understanding the Special Needs, Awareness, and Communications of the Dying.* Simon and Schuster, 2012

People think chaplains bring God into the room with them, but God is not static electricity—God is alternating current. God is the spark that leaps the synapse between two souls. It is when a connection opens up between me and the patient or the patient's family that I feel the charge, and it goes both ways. Which is why, while it is often sad, hospice work is not—as people seem to assume it must be—depressing; in fact, it is often joyful.

We prayed part of the *Mi Sheibeirach* together: *Mi shebeirach avoteinu, m'kor habracha l'imoteinu.* May the Source of Strength, who blessed the ones who came before us, give us the courage to make our lives a blessing. Though this is traditionally a prayer for healing, I like to pray it with the families of the dying, because it captures my beliefs about suffering and death. God didn't "take" these women's husband and brother; he died because he had cancer. If his death is to have meaning, it will be because of the blessing bestowed by his memory upon the lives of the living. Give us the courage.

-Chapter 19-

Troubling Grace[xiv]

Religious people want there to be meaning in everything. Randomness is hard on us: that things happen for no reason sometimes brings us closer than we want to be to the possibility that we're not central to much of anything, and most of us are still too wedded to our ancient anthropocentrism to give that up. —Barbara Crafton, *Jesus Wept: When Faith and Depression Meet*

When we are no longer able to change a situation…we are challenged to change ourselves. —Viktor Frankl, *Man's Search for Meaning*

✝ ✝ ✝

Some time around the second grade I was traumatized by an educational movie about Beethoven. I remember sitting in the music classroom at my elementary school, hearing the cinematic re-creation of the humming in the composer's ears as his deafness advanced, and his anguished voice asking God why He would give the gift of music to one destined not to hear it. Believing that his gifts as a composer meant something, and that his hearing loss was equally fraught with meaning, the irreconcilability of meanings tortured him, perhaps even more than the deafness itself.

His unanswerable question nourished in me a terror that would plague me into middle age: the terror of the possibility that the things that happen mean something. The notion that neither Beethoven's ability nor his disability meant a cotton-pickin' thing is so deeply unsettling as to render it well-nigh inadmissible, yet the opposing position—that either or both *did* have meaning—raises the specter of Divine indifference, negligence or downright cruelty.

Though I am experiencing more presbyaudia than I like, I do not appear to be in immediate danger of going deaf—but I did struggle for years with vocation and meaning in my career. The facts of the matter are these: 1) I can write worthwhile music, and 2) I cannot get it performed. Because I believed there was meaning in Fact #1—that I was "called" to be a composer—I spent years in fruitless agony over Fact #2: why would God bestow the gift of music on someone who was destined to go unheard? Yet both are just facts, and the question of what they *mean* is a non-starter because they don't *mean* a blessed thing. So it is up to me, the facts being what they are, to decide what to do with the bundle of desires and predilections I blithely call "myself"; trying to derive meaning from the meaningless and wanting things to be other than they are just eats up your life.

So when I see people in danger of inflicting the same injuries on themselves as I did, I want to stop them, warn them off their self-destructive course. Earlier this year, I read this Facebook status update posted by a friend and former student who is a talented writer and sci-fi/fantasy übergeek:

(Xxxx Xxxxx) got rejected by (xxxxx.com) for a position writing about Star Wars. WRITING. About STAR WARS. If I can't get that job, I really don't think I have much chance in this world...

Oh no, I thought; she thinks it *means* something that she didn't get the job. And her friends' comments, trying to make sense of the slight—explain it away—aren't helping. Not wanting to see this smart, talented, creative young woman become bogged down in bootless speculation about meaning, I decided it was time to put in my own unsolicited oar. I wasn't about to tell her that hard work and talent are inevitably rewarded and she must surely succeed some day, that everything happens for a reason, that America is the Land of Opportunity and God Has a Plan For Your Life, because that's all bullshit. The truth, as I see it, is actually far simpler than all that.

Don't look too hard for meaning; there is a lot less of it than we think, and the search for it burdens us. Sometimes things just suck.

Her response followed quickly.

It's rather amazing how that comment was depressing and encouraging at the same time…

Except that it isn't amazing, really. "Joy and woe," as Blake knew, "are woven fine, / A clothing for the soul divine." The older you get, the more you realize that both are always present. They are inextricable warp and weft; we put them on like garments and they take our shape for a while, then they fall away. They, too, do not mean anything.

I have a friend who grew up in the church—who majored in church music, in fact—and turned her back on it when her three-year-old niece died. What could I say to her? In the years since she told me about it, I have said nothing. I don't how to make what I want to say—that whatever meaning there is in her niece's death resides, not in the event itself, but in the responses to it of the people who loved her—leap the synapse that exists between one who has suffered such a thing and one who has not. Perhaps it ought not to be leapt. I also don't know what she was taught to believe about such things; if anyone were to tell me to accept that my child's death was part of a divine plan, I might well walk away, too.

We want to find meaning in things. When Sri Ramakrishna was dying of throat cancer, his devotees tried to make sense of his illness, some by believing that he had willed it on himself to bring his devotees together, some believing that the Divine Mother had caused it for reasons of her own.

But the young rationalists, led by Narendra [later known to the world as Swami Vivekananda] *refused to ascribe a supernatural cause to a natural phenomenon. They believed that the Master's body, a material thing, was subject, like all other material things, to physical laws.* (M)

I love Vivekananda's steady clear-sightedness. It takes courage to stop looking for meaning in events and take on instead the task of bestowing meaning by the way we live in the face of them. His stern pursuance of reason, and impatience with what he called "superstition" and "beings above the clouds" make a bracing tonic for anyone caught in the God Has a Plan for Your Life trap.

We have desires, and we call them promptings; abilities, and we call them vocations; we parse them, and call it discernment. We make choices, and navigate our way through their consequences. Things happen to us, and they do not have meaning in themselves—we endow them with meaning by our responses to them. In a Catholic church in rural Lancaster County, Pennsylvania, the celebrant announced that a beloved former priest of the parish, who was dying of cancer, was "offering up" his suffering for that community. Never having heard of such a thing outside of Irish literature, I was stunned when I realized what it really meant: by voluntarily joining his suffering with Jesus', the priest was refusing to be a victim of his circumstances, turning instead a thing that had happened to him into a freely-offered instrument of redemption. Love, as Evelyn Underhill put it, makes all the difference between an execution and a martyrdom.

The Devil trembles when human beings know "that horrors may be in store for (them,) and are praying for the virtues wherewith to meet them." (Lewis, *The Screwtape Letters: How a Senior Devil Instructs a Junior Devil in the Art of Temptation*) Things may happen to us—even fatal things—but spiritual death is not visited upon us; we bring it upon ourselves.

Phillip, the semi-autobiographical protagonist of Somerset Maugham's novel *Of Human Bondage*, met a dissipated and largely unpublished poet in Paris named Cronshaw, who gave Phillip a remnant of a Persian carpet. The carpet, Cronshaw told him, held in it the answer to the meaning of life. Phillip kept the remnant for many years, through titanic struggles, repeated failures and almost relentless suffering as he tried to find what the world called "success" in life. One day, long after the carpet fragment had been lost, Phillip realized, with the abruptness of revelation, the truth that had eluded him for so many years: life does not have any meaning.

His insignificance was turned to power, and he felt himself suddenly equal with the cruel fate which had seemed to persecute him; for, if life was meaningless, the world was robbed of its cruelty... Failure was unimportant and success amounted to nothing...(T)hat was why

Cronshaw, he imagined, had given him the Persian rug. As the weaver elaborated his pattern for no end but the pleasure of his aesthetic sense, so might a man live his life...Out of the manifold events of his life, his deeds, his feelings, his thoughts, he might make a design, regular, elaborate, complicated, or beautiful... There was one pattern, the most obvious, perfect, and beautiful, in which a man was born, grew to manhood, married, produced children, toiled for his bread, and died; but there were others, intricate and wonderful, in which happiness did not enter and in which success was not attempted; and in them might be discovered a more troubling grace...His life had seemed horrible when it was measured by its happiness, but now he seemed to gather strength as he realised that it might be measured by something else. Happiness mattered as little as pain. They came in, both of them, as all the other details of his life came in, to the elaboration of the design. (314)

Whatever meaning, whatever beauty there is in life resides in our living of it, and not in the events of life themselves. Sloppy biblical interpretation often involves *eisegesis,* the "reading in" of meaning to the text. I have spent most of my days doing a similar thing: reading meaning into life. But meaning is not in life any more than a pattern is in the threads; we must weave our carpets for ourselves.

[xiv] "Troubling Grace" first appeared in *Elephant Journal* under the title "Sometimes Things Just Suck," on December 21, 2011, in a slightly different form. Used here by permission.

-Chapter 20-

Karma: It's Nothing Personal[xv]

Man's life in the world is bound by his actions. –Bhagavad Gita
15:2

* * *

When I was a kid, I used to get angry at inanimate objects.

I would dial our rotary telephone too fast, and become incensed when the call did not go through. I would shift gears on my bicycle too quickly and grumble when the chain jumped off the sprockets. I would muscle the lawnmower through tall grass and grouse when it became clogged.

Though I cannot reconstruct my exact state of mind at the time, it seems that I attributed moral agency to machines, and interpreted their negligent or intentional thwarting of my purposes as conscious acts. My father tried over and over to convince me that it wasn't a moral issue— that that was simply the way the machines worked. But I seem to have been sure, at some level, that they were doing it on purpose.

Interestingly, it was this unarticulated belief that kept me from changing the way I behaved in order to change what happened to me. As long as I believed the telephone could have worked the way I wanted it to if it chose, its demand that I dial it in a certain way seemed arbitrary, and I refused to comply. I wasn't responsible for what happened to me—the mean old phone was.

Does this sound familiar? If you were reared in a Christian environment, it may. In fact, it may even if you weren't, because the belief in a personal God around which Western culture is built encourages us to believe, consciously or unconsciously, that the consequences of our actions are meted out by a discriminating entity bent on rewarding or punishing us. And you may have noticed that, as often as not, a rule-bound religious upbringing oriented toward pleasing a heavenly judge is about as much of a deterrent to bad behavior as capital punishment, and maybe less.

Whenever I hear people say that "everything happens for a reason," I want to ask them whether they mean that every event has a *cause*, or that every event has a *purpose*. I suspect that most often, they mean the latter: that things happen because "the universe" wants them to for reasons of its own. But I am here to dispute that: things happen because of what we do—not as a result of any conscious moral agency, but because that's simply the way the machine works. Every action has an equal and opposite reaction, and every event is the result of causation. Garbage in, garbage out.

Of course, the obvious question is *why* the machine works that way, and so many answers have been posited for that one that I will not attempt to answer it here. And I hasten to add that many of the most enlightened people I have known have had a deep, experientially informed faith in a personal God, and that simply has to mean something. But I am nevertheless going to insist that, when what goes around comes around, it does so not because God sent it, but because that's simply the way the machine works.

This is the doctrine of *karma* as I understand it, and it has been immensely liberating for me because it has allowed me to experience what happens to me principally as the result of my own actions. Before, I was like the kids in a cartoon I once saw, marching around the kitchen banging on pots until one of them said, "I wish mom would tell us to stop; I'm getting tired." Now, responsibility rests with me—not because anybody says so, but because that's just the way the machine works. Neither can one act without consequences, because the mechanism is simply not set up that way. As you sow, so shall you reap. (See Galatians 6:7-8)

So, when the old Charles Wesley hymn entitled "A Thought on Judgment" (first published in 1763, now in the public domain) asks. . .

> *And must I be to judgment brought,*
> *And answer in that day,*
> *For every vain and idle thought,*
> *And every word I say?*

. . .*karma* answers Yes; not because God is watching you and writing everything down in His book, but because every thought, word and deed creates *samskaras* (impressions) in the *chitta* (mind-stuff), and sends out ripples into the world, that are simply going to have to work themselves out.

> *Yes, every secret of my heart,*
> *Shall shortly be made known,*
> *And I receive my just desert*
> *For all that I have done.*

Yes, says *karma*—that's absolutely true. And whether your belief in a personal God who knows when you've been bad or good so be good for goodness' sake is explicit or implicit, up-front or deep beneath the surface, this is—as strange as it may sound—very good news.

[xv] "Karma: It's Nothing Personal" first appeared in *Elephant Journal* on August 29, 2012, in a slightly different form. Used here by permission.

-Chapter 21-

Bumper Karma[xvi]

[T]here are in fact innocent victims in the harsh reality of the world, and our hearts go out to them and their families...It is the senselessness of such events that hits us hardest and this cannot be covered over with bad metaphysics. Life is precious because it is fragile and fleeting.
—Julian Walker

* * *

A younger friend of mine recently died of a rare and fast-moving cancer.

It wasn't her fault.

People want so badly for there to be reasons for things—and of course, everything does "happen for a reason," inasmuch as every event has a *cause*. This is not the same, however, as saying that every event has a *purpose*. The latter presupposes conscious agency where, I am here to argue, none necessarily exists. My friend died because some cells in her body were induced, by some combination of environmental stimuli and genetic predisposition, to mutate and reproduce out of control. That's it. The cause *is* the reason.

The Gospel of Luke puts it this way:

Now there were some present at that time who told Jesus about the Galileans whose blood Pilate had mixed with their sacrifices. Jesus answered, "Do you think that these Galileans were worse sinners than all the other Galileans because they suffered this way? I tell you, no! But unless you repent, you too will all perish. Or those eighteen who died when the tower in Siloam fell on them—do you think they were more guilty than all the others living in Jerusalem? I tell you, no! But unless you repent, you too will all perish. " (Luke 13:2-5, NIV)

The people crushed by the tower, or slaughtered by the Romans, did not bring those disasters on themselves by anything they did "wrong." They may have contributed to what lawyers call the "proximate cause" of their sufferings—by being in the wrong place at the wrong time, for instance. But the "ultimate cause"—the legal term for what "really" made something happen, if you follow the causal chain back far enough—usually does not exist. At any rate, not in the glib way people mean when they say "everything happens for a reason."

And yet, what we do does certainly seem to "come back to us." Jesus told his hearers that, while the individual sufferers in these two incidents did nothing to deserve their deaths, unless Israel as a whole changed its ways, it would meet with a similar fate— which, of course, it did, when the Romans destroyed the Temple and drove the people into exile.

Suppose, for instance, that something toxic in the environment caused my friend's cancer. That wasn't her fault. But unless we stop fouling our planetary nest, we are all going to meet a similar fate.

Karma, you see, is a *complex system.*

Think, for instance, of a bathtub. Water flows in from the spigot, and out through the drain. If your goal is to fill the bathtub, you increase the rate of *inflow* by turning up the faucet, and/or decrease the rate of *outflow* by plugging the drain. Your *stock* will then increase. If you want to drain the bathtub, reverse the process: increase *outflow,* and/or decrease *inflow,* and your *stock* will eventually vanish.

(Meadows 8)

Now suppose this is a swimming pool, with multiple sources of inflow—say, a faucet and rain—and outflow—for instance, evaporation, splashing and a drain. Multiple inflow and outflow sources rapidly increase the complexity of the system.

Now imagine that we are dealing with, say, the Tucson water table. Between 1945 and 2005, the groundwater level under Tucson plunged 170 feet. Evidently, the complexity of the system—including rainfall, pumping, climate change, and conflicting human interests—has resulted in a dramatic loss of equilibrium in the system. (Rillito River Project) Moreover, if I lived in Tucson, I might do everything humanly possible to promote responsible water use, and still run out of water myself. And without large-scale change, the whole system—and other systems with which it is interconnected will be catastrophically altered.

Unless you repent, you too will all perish.

I am here to challenge the assumption that there is always a direct causal link between what we do and what happens to us on an individual basis; I'm here to say that, while *our thoughts, words and deeds do come back to us, not everything that comes to us is the direct result of our own thoughts, words and deeds.*

Back to the bathtub. According to Tantric thought, we each have a "stock" of karma, the *samcita*, or "accumulated" karma, comprising the sum of all karmas accrued during all our lifetimes. Through the "inflow" of our birth, we bring that portion of our total karma that we are meant to work out in this lifetime—the *prarabdha*, or "undertaken" karma. But there is another karmic inflow: the *kriyamana*, or "being done" karma, the karma we are making right now. Our thoughts, words and deeds continually generate new karma, which flows into the karmic bathtub.

All the while, we are, though spiritual practice and good deeds, doing our utmost to make the karmic outflow outstrip the inflow, so that our stock of karma diminishes, and we "drain the bathtub."

Sometimes, karma is worked out comparatively quickly, resulting in no net increase.

Agami karma ("next") is the result of actions that will be worked out within this lifetime and does not contribute to samcita karma. The criminal justice system, when it functions properly, is an example of agami karma in action. Agami karma is the closest to the pop culture understanding of "what goes around comes around"...Unfortunately, it doesn't always work that way! (Boccio)

No, it doesn't. And I'm going to take it a step further: my college roommate's three-year-old was not responsible for his own death from cancer at age three— not from anything he did in this life, nor anything he may have done in his previous life. What if *samcita karma* does wait in the *svarga lokah*, or causal body—the "energy body" that survives from one incarnation to the next—for the soul to be reborn so it can work itself out? What does the death of a three-year-old work out? For himself, or his parents? What was learned? What was atoned for? How much fiery *tapas,* or spiritual motive power, can be generated for burning off karma by the immolation of a toddler? The idea simply doesn't bear scrutiny.

And my friend didn't do anything to deserve to die of her cancer, either.

Because if you think about it, there are simply too many variables in play; our karmas bump and jostle and slosh into each other like brimming beer mugs on a tray.

Did the victims of the April, 2012 Oklahoma tornadoes deserve to die? I tell you, no. But unless we do something, and soon, to stop the disastrous course upon which we have set our planet, more and more of us are going to die that way, because of our own, and everybody else's, actions.

Unless you repent, you too will all perish.

Too much of what one hears about karma makes it sound like a simple drain-spigot problem in a private bathtub—a simple, closed system. But it isn't. We're more like all the various features at a water park—many, many inflows, myriad outflows, and endless opportunities for our stocks to become intermingled and contaminated. We each have our karmas, but so does everybody else, and our karmas bash into each other like bumper cars. It's a system complex beyond imagination.

So if one cannot necessarily find meaning in individual events, does that mean everything is meaningless? A closer look at what we mean by "system" might help answer that.

"A system," wrote Donella Meadows, "is an interconnected set of elements that is coherently organized in a way that achieves something." (Meadows 1) I have been arguing against the idea that a conscious agency is at work in every event, but that doesn't necessarily mean that the system as a whole doesn't achieve anything. And I think Swami Vivekananda had as clear a sense as anyone of the goal of the universal system as a whole.

"Come unto Me, all ye that labour and are heavy laden, and I will give you rest." This is the voice that is leading us forward. Man has heard it—and is hearing it—all through the ages... Some inner voice tells us that we are free. But if we attempt to realise that freedom, to make it manifest, we find the difficulties almost insuperable. Yet, in spite of that it insists on asserting itself inwardly, "I am free, I am free." ... That voice has been heard by everyone, whether he knows it or not...It may not be in the same language or the same form of speech, but in some form or other, that voice calling for freedom has been with us. Yes, we are born here on account of that voice; every one of our movements is for that. We are all rushing towards freedom, we are all following that voice, whether we know it or not; as the children of the village were attracted by the music of the flute-player, so we are all following the music of the voice without knowing it. (Vivekananda, *Jnana Yoga* 70)*

We rush and struggle and stumble toward freedom, as the universe is designed to make us do. We do terrible things to ourselves and each other. Our every action comes back, ultimately, to ourselves, but also to anyone else who happens to be in the way. Sometimes we are the actor, and sometimes we are the acted-upon. Often, things that happen make no sense at all, happening for no discernable reason at all, and either malevolence visited them upon us or indifference looked on, bored, and both choices are terrifying.

But it is a false dilemma, because "the whole creation has been groaning as in the pains of childbirth right up to the present time." (Romans 8:22) And birth is painful. Always, the system as a whole is driving us all into the great cosmic bottleneck through which, ultimately, we shall all pass, and be free.

[xvi] "Bumper Karma" first appeared in *Elephant Journal* on May 31, 2013, in a slightly different form. Used here by permission.

-Chapter 22-

Participation Trophy[xvii]

So God created man in his own image, in the image of God he created him; male and female he created them. —Genesis 1:27

* * *

"Realized there are 10 movies nominated for Best Pic," read a friend's Facebook status. "Looks like all the kids who got 'participation trophies' are now grown up."

The implication being, I suppose, that receiving 'participation trophies'—or simply growing up in a culture that gave prizes to kids just for showing up—has turned a generation into entitled hellions. But while there may be a cohort of young people out there with an inflated sense of what they have coming to them, I think the trophies have become a lightning rod. First, where older kids are concerned, they hardly seem capable of inflating anyone's self-concept.

> ...(T)he expression "trophy kids" misses a rather important point: It sucks to get one of those participation trophies... Every time I looked at them, I felt embarrassed. They were reminders of my ineptitude, because I knew I didn't earn them. No young athlete with any sense of perspective would mistake those trophies for genuine celebrations of accomplishment. My classmates and I joked about them; we rolled our eyes when they were passed out at end-of-season pizza parties. (Bosch)

Second, some people still think the trophies are good for the littlest kids—especially those who come from less-nurturing home environments. If you'd never been told in your life that you were good at anything, imagine what a difference a trophy could make. It's fashionable to grouse that self-esteem has to be earned. "Self-esteem does not lead to success in life," said one anti-trophy pundit; "Self-discipline and self-control do." (Reiss) But no one can earn anything if they don't believe they have any personal capital. Kids need to believe they have a self worth controlling. You have to prime the pump a little.

Having said that, I'm not prepared to weigh in on whether we ought to give participation trophies or not—but I do think the controversy surrounding them is beside the point where self-esteem is concerned. If a positive self-image is the goal, these trophies are decidedly downstream ministry. (Downstream ministry, as I heard someone put it once, "reaches into the river of despair and pulls out drowning souls," while upstream ministry "finds out who's throwing them in and makes them stop.") I'm interested in why kids come to school needing a plastic trophy to feel good about themselves in the first place.

I've known people who actually believe that self-esteem is a bad thing—that we really are caught in a Calvinist nightmare in which a keen sense of our own depravity is all that can save us from self-indulgence, indolence and moral decay. And while of course an appropriate sense of our shortcomings is essential if we are to overcome them, the sins that I-am-a-worm-and-no-man self-loathing is meant to forestall are not the result of self-love. We take it for granted, for instance, that over-indulgence of others is not really showing them love, yet automatically identify self-indulgence with self-love. But that's not what self-indulgence is. Anyone who's ever been or known an addicted person, for instance, knows that people don't indulge themselves out of self-love, but in a desperate bid to fill the "god-shaped hole" inside them. People are lazy because they do not believe industry worthwhile, immoral because they see themselves as bad. Self-esteem is the foundation of self-discipline and self-control, not a hindrance to them.

"I do think I see some shred of goodness in John Proctor," said the hard-pressed Puritan in Arthur Miller's play, *The Crucible.* "Not enough to weave a banner with, but white enough to keep it from such dogs." Proctor was lucky; those who see no shred of goodness in themselves do not bother.

"Self-love, not sex, is his woe," screamed the headline about a sports analyst in the wake of a sex scandal. (MacIntosh) But grown men don't cheat on their wives with 22-year-olds because they love themselves—they do it because they see no shred of goodness in themselves to keep white.

It would probably help if we had a more precise word for "self-love." The Countess Olivia in Shakespeare's *Twelfth Night* told her killjoy steward Malvolio (also a Puritan) that he was "sick" with it—but Malvolio's supercilious self-righteousness, browbeating and social ambition are really the stuff of self-loathing, not self-love. If he really had a healthy love for himself, he wouldn't need to look down his nose at everybody. We are called upon to love our neighbors as we love ourselves.

Amy Miller, an associate professor of biology at the University of Alabama at Huntsville, opened fire during a department meeting in February of 2010, killing three of her colleagues.

It wasn't her first violent episode, either. In 2002, she plead guilty to a charge of misdemeanor assault after punching a woman in the head at an International House of Pancakes because the woman had taken the last booster seat for her child. (Dewan)

If someone punches a stranger in the head over something like that, all the while screaming "I am Dr. Amy Bishop!" it isn't because she loves herself too much; if she loved herself, giving up the last booster in the IHOP wouldn't diminish her personally. She used her name, and whatever accomplishments and human value it supposedly represented, as a kind of kryptonite against those she perceived as a threat and, alarmed when it didn't work, lashed out violently in order, not to get a booster seat, but to avoid facing the real emptiness of that carefully-constructed identity. If she later shot six members of her department who had denied her tenure, again, it wasn't because she loved herself too much. She doesn't even know who she is, and the possibility that the self she built out of academic ambition and a fudged résumé may not be real or meaningful terrifies her. She would kill to defend that self, rather than face the emptiness she fears underneath it.

"Go down low, low, low as you can go," said microbiologist and accused anthrax mailer Bruce Ivins, "then dig forever, and you'll find me, my psyche." (Shane) Human beings made in the image of God mistreat each other because we think, not too much of ourselves, but too little.

This is the real problem that participation trophies—and all other worldly awards and rewards—fail to address. Do people who really know that they are God's children *need* prizes or 'retail therapy", or *need* so badly for things to be a certain way that they will scream at a public official in a town hall meeting, or *need* a drink, or dismiss rural people as "shitkickers", or *need* the acceptance represented by tenure so much that they will kill if denied it? A kid who knows she is made in the Image of God does not need a participation trophy, while a kid who doesn't will not be helped by one where help is needed most. And I worry that we are teaching kids to want tokens of recognition— which are not bad things in themselves—as a substitute for teaching them who they really are: the Pearl of Great Price. The things we want are notoriously bad stewards of our identities and happiness. Where your treasure is, there your heart will be also. (Matthew 6:21)

The importance of self-esteem to spiritual growth may be hard to see because so many stories of saints and ascetics often appear at first to be chronicles of masochistic self-loathing. But I have come to believe that self denial can actually be a sign of a true and healthy self-love. We deny things to our children because we love them, to teach them to delay gratification lest they trade in what they want most for what they want now. Though Madison Avenue would have us believe that we should indulge ourselves because we're "worth it," that isn't actually why we indulge ourselves most of the time. We indulge ourselves because we think the desired object or experience will fill our inner void. But when we are really on our game, knowing that we are "worth it" can lead us to practice loving self-denial.

Nikos Kazantzakis's novel *St. Francis* includes a number of incidents which, while they never actually occurred in real life, are much in keeping with the spirit of Francis and his followers. In one alarming episode, Francis's disciple Brother Giles stands up in a public square with a basket of figs and announces that he will give one to whoever slaps him once, while anyone who slaps him twice will receive two. Things fall out as you'd expect, and Giles rapturously reports to Francis the success of the experiment.

I had a strong, and strongly ambivalent, reaction to this story. On the one hand, the apparent untrammeled self-hatred of it is appalling, especially when portrayed as an aid to spiritual progress. But on the other hand, I found—and still find—the story powerfully compelling. I was convinced that there was some genuine wisdom in it (and in similar events in the actual lives of the early Franciscans) but, couched at it was in such off-putting terms, I couldn't get at it until many years later, when I had a personal epiphany about suffering and self-worth.

I was in the kitchen (as I often am when I have epiphanies, my other revelatory venue being the shower) with my infant Sophie screaming her head off on my shoulder, and my toddler Clare wrapped around my leg crying "Uppy! Uppy!" with all the apocalyptic pathos of which toddlers are capable. Having frantically tried everything I could think of to make the screaming stop, I suddenly stopped myself, as the dawning realization lit up within me: *It just doesn't matter what I want!*

When that thought came to me, I stood still and laughed out loud. My children were not going to stop screaming no matter what I did, it didn't matter that it was making me miserable, and it was all OK! We expend a staggering amount of psychic calories in self-assertion, in defending our right to exist and be right. If people don't do what we want, we assume that it *means* something about *us*. We need to win in order to prove that we are good. This is the real root of self-will: not self-love, but insecurity and self-doubt. It doesn't have to matter so much what we want if we know who we are.

"Everything that we do has a kind of basic mantra behind it, like 'What about me?'" (Tyagananda) It's exhausting and, like beating your head against a wall, it feels *so* good when you stop. But the absolutely indispensable thing that enables us to stop the mantra without falling into despair—to really believe that we will continue to matter after we stop inwardly screaming that we do—is self-esteem: the unshakeable realization that we are Children of God, made in God's image, and nothing bar nothing can change or diminish that. Your slap cannot touch me; here's your fig.

After Paul and some other apostles were hailed before the Sanhedrin and flogged, they left "rejoicing because they had been counted worthy of suffering disgrace for the Name." (Acts 5:41) This passage astonished me when I first read it, and still convicts me of pettiness and ingratitude whenever I catch myself sulking because someone has failed to show me what I consider due deference. The apostles knew that their real selves remained untouched by flogging, and that "disgrace" in the eyes of the Council did not make a particle of difference to their real lives, "hidden with Christ in God." (Colossians 3:3) If that isn't self-esteem—being beyond the dirty devices and brute broken nails of the world—I can't imagine what is.

Maybe it would help if we used the Sanskrit word *maitri* in preference to the loaded "self-esteem." *Maitri*, as Buddhist teacher Pema Chödrön explains, "is translated in a lot of ways, maybe most commonly as *love*, but the way (my teacher) Chogyam Trungpa Rinpoche translated it was *unconditional friendliness* and in particular *unconditional friendliness to oneself*." (Chodron)

We can be unconditionally friendly to someone

without indulging them, or failing to hold them to account, or telling them flattering untruths. I think the early Franciscan cultivation of radical humility was, at the same time, an affirmation of *maitri*. You may slap me, and it doesn't actually mean a thing. My children may continue to scream, and it doesn't diminish me in the least. Maybe Jesus tells us to turn the other cheek because He knows who we are better than we do.

A friend of mine used to be absolutely frantic for "success" in the pop music world. One morning as we drove to a festival we were performing at, he attempted to stick a label on a demo CD to give to someone he had heard might be there. The car hit a bump, and the CD was ruined. My friend fell into dejection; a potential opportunity had been lost!

Some five years later, I walked into his studio and congratulated him on being named Artist of the Month on one of the XM radio stations. He shrugged; "It's not like my life is any different," he said. During those intervening years, my friend had learned where his self-worth actually lay. He still works hard and is still doing well, but the desperation is gone. "Succeeding" is a matter of making a satisfying living in his chosen field, and no longer a matter of proving his personal value.

The trouble is that we look for the trophies—we take the world so much at its word in its estimate of our value. Happily, a little distraction can help draw our attention away from our carefully-constructed identities and what we believe are their needs, allowing us to remember who we really are. For instance, a college classmate of mine who has built a successful career as an actor told me how much perspective fatherhood has given him.

"I'll be waiting to go into an audition," he said, "and

I'll suddenly remember: 'Oh, right—this *isn't* the most important thing in the world!'" Fatherhood is. So he relaxes. And interestingly—as many of you reading this can probably attest—this kind of knowledge of one's true value and identity is, far from being a handicap, actually an asset. Nothing makes the universe hide the keys like desperation. A person who has seen the Image of God in himself doesn't get hooked as easily, doesn't need so badly to fill up any internal void—and it shows.

Growing up, I was always told how brilliant I was. Although I was a classic underachiever, IQ tests and the like seemed to bear out those early assessments. As my later life failed to deliver the trophies that all the early prognostications seemed to have promised, I became increasingly desperate to succeed at something, *anything;* it became unthinkable that I should never have anything to "show" for all those brains I supposedly had.

My wife hates it when I put a pot of tea in the oven to keep warm, because it's such an inefficient use of energy. I often identified with the oven: though I never lacked for work to do, it never seemed like the work was worth all I had to give to it. I had placed all the eggs of my self-worth in the basket of success, and not until very late did I begin to believe that I could be happy in any other way.

This is why we need to stop telling people that "God has a plan for your life." For most of my adult life I have felt like Willem in the movie *Mallrats,* staring at a Magic Eye picture in which everyone can see the hidden image but him. Where's the plan, I said for years; show me the plan! It all seemed so cruel; if God has a plan for my life, why does one thing after another not work out? "Do you even believe in God any more?" my wife finally asked. "It would hurt a lot less if I didn't," I told her.

I have come to believe that God doesn't have a plan for my life any more than I do for my children's lives. All I want for my children is to know that they are a part of me and I love them—that they are the Pearl of Great Price, made in the image of God. I just want them to be happy whether they set the world on fire or not. I want them to have *maitri* and be at peace with themselves. If God has a plan, that has to be it.

When my mom, dying of cancer, was coming to grips with the impossibility of returning to teaching, she said to me, "If I'm not a teacher, what am I?" A Woodrow Wilson Fellow, she had for years been offered lab assistant and other low-status jobs because of her gender. Her graduate program of choice didn't even accept applications from women at the time. By dint of brains, unremitting hard work and sheer doggedness, she became head of the biology department at an upstate New York college.

An adult child of alcoholics, she had, I believe, spent her whole life establishing the self-worth that her childhood had failed to give her. Even with her strong Christian faith, she had allowed her identity to become bound up with her profession to the extent that no longer teaching left her in danger of thinking herself a non-person. If I could have that moment back, here's what I would tell her:

> You are a Child of God; you share spiritual DNA with Jesus, the Image of the Invisible God in Whose image you are also made. You are a seat of the divine spark. You are beloved of your family and respected by your peers and those are very good things, but they are not who you are. You have your trophies, and you earned them, but they do not matter in the end. You are the Pearl of Great Price.

And I would tell her what Joshua Ben Levi, a Rabbi of the Talmud, said:

A procession of angels pass before each human being wherever he goes, proclaiming, "Make way for the image of God."

---

xvii "Participation Trophy" first appeared in *Elephant Journal* on September 28, 2011, in a slightly different form. Used here by permission.

-Chapter 23-

The Nursery Magic[xviii]

> "Real isn't how you are made," said the Skin Horse. "It's a thing that happens to you..."
>
> "Does it hurt?" asked the Rabbit.
>
> "Sometimes," said the Skin Horse for he was always truthful. "When you are Real you don't mind being hurt."
>
> "Does it happen all at once, like being wound up," he asked, "or but by bit?"
>
> "It doesn't happen all at once," said the Skin Horse. "You become. It takes a long time. That's why it doesn't often happen to people who break easily, or have sharp edges, or who have to be carefully kept. Generally, by the time you are Real, most of your fur has been loved off, and your eyes drop out and you get loose in the joints and very shabby. But these things don't matter at all, because once you are Real you can't be ugly, except to people who don't understand."
>
> "I suppose you are Real? Said the Rabbit...
>
> "Once you are Real you can't become unreal again. It lasts for always."
>
> The Rabbit sighed...He wished that he could become Real without these uncomfortable things happening to him.
>
> —Margery Williams, The Velveteen Rabbit, or How Toys Become Real[19]

* * *

My second daughter, Sophie, didn't sleep through the night until she was two and half years old. For the first

---

[19] First published in 1922, The Velveteen Rabbit is in the public domain.

few months, she was (read: "we were") up every ninety minutes during the night. My wife Allison, through sheer fatigue, turned a ghastly gray-green color that alarmed me, and my own mental fog garnered me the worst student evaluations that semester in my entire ten years of teaching.

During the infancy of my two girls, Allison expressed more than once her surprise at how I managed to rise to the occasion of fatherhood. I was surprised myself—I discovered hidden reserves I had no idea I had, and began to feel like a TARDIS—those spaceship/time machines from Doctor Who that are worlds larger on the inside than on the outside.

Fatherhood has been an exercise in Becoming Real. My children delight in pointing out how much grey has appeared in my beard. But the "uncomfortable things" of fatherhood, like the ones the Skin Horse described, are keepers. The Sisyphusean hamster wheel of chores, the logistical difficulties of leading a normal life with a toddler to preserve from grievous bodily harm (Sophie still managed to break a leg—on my watch—when she was eleven months old,) the weird abjectness of having a screaming infant on the shoulder and a screaming toddler on the leg, the nightmares about strollers rolling down embankments, the terror when I looked around at a block party at the empty spot where my 18-month-old Sophie had been a moment ago, my fear of the coming years of peer brutality that no parent's vigilance can ward off—they are all worth it. As often as I ask myself why on earth anyone would open themselves up to the profound vulnerability of having small people utterly dependent upon them, I wouldn't trade the experiences in for anything. They have moved me farther down the Road to Real than my whole pre-fatherhood life had taken me.

I had read many times the passage from the Gospel of Matthew in which Jesus reminds his hearers that none of them, if their children asked for bread, would give them a stone, or a serpent if they asked for an egg—and if they, who were evil, knew how to give good gifts to their children, how much more would God give good things to those who ask? Candidly, I had always suspected that, once I had children, I would discover that that was arrant malarkey. God loves me more than I love my children? It doesn't make a shred of sense; what could be more counter-intuitive? And yet, against all reason, I knew the first time I held Clare that it was all true, and parenthood was a window into the heart of God.

I remember trying to change Clare's diaper as she screamed and kicked and twisted in protest; I found myself yelling at her, "I AM TRYING TO HELP YOU! IF YOU WOULD JUST STOP YELLING AND HOLD STILL YOU WOULD UNDERSTAND!"

And suddenly, I stopped yelling myself, thunderstruck by the realization that I could be God, talking to Scott. Quit your bitching and thrashing—I am trying to help you!

I know an elderly woman who is one of those people who lifts your spirits every time you see her. During one of my Eucharistic Visitations, we were talking about the recessed economy, and she told me of her memories of the Great Depression, when Philadelphia's West River Drive was lined with mile after mile of tent city, and people came to her parents' back door every single day looking for a handout of food which was never refused. When I caught sight of some black-and-white photos of young men in uniform, she told me about her sons, two of whom she has survived—one of whom she was with, holding his hand, as he died of pancreatic cancer. And when she says that no experience, even grief and loss, ever goes to waste—her, I can hear, with shame at my own breathtaking ingratitude.

It doesn't often happen to people who break easily, or have sharp edges, or who have to be carefully kept.

So often when my girls were babies, I remembered a sermon I'd heard years ago in which the priest told us that of course, he had expected to love his children—but nothing could have possibly prepared him for the overwhelming flood of all-consuming love they would awaken in him. And nothing could have prepared him for the pain of hearing them say Daddy, I lost my job; Daddy, I'm an alcoholic; Daddy, I'm getting a divorce. If you want to get in touch with the Passion of God, he told us, you just go and have yourself some children.

Why would God open Himself up like that? Make Himself so vulnerable? Why in the world would God do that?

The Spirit, poet Mary Oliver tells us, wants to be "more than pure light that shines where no one is." Maybe God created us in order to experience the Nursery Magic of the Skin Horse: to become more Real.

[xviii] "The Nursery Magic (Becoming Real)" first appeared in *Elephant Journal* on July 24, 2010, in a slightly different form. Used here by permission.

PART III

You Can Observe a Lot by Watching

"O you who reach after perfection and are tempted to be discouraged by what you read about the lives of the saints and what works of piety prescribe! Who are daunted by exalted notions of perfection! It is for your consolation that God wishes me to write this." —Jean-Pierre de Caussade, *The Sacrament of the Present Moment*

"Just a little opening up of the heart is enough." — Brother Lawrence, *The Practice of the Presence of God*

-Chapter 24-

Attention Means Attention

[A] student said to Master Ichu, 'Please write for me something of great wisdom.'
Master Ichu picked up his brush and wrote one word: 'Attention.'
The student said, 'Is that all?'
The master wrote, 'Attention, Attention.'
The student became irritable. "That doesn't seem profound or subtle to me.'
In response, Master Ichu wrote simply, 'Attention. Attention. Attention.'
In frustration, the student demanded, 'What does this word attention mean?'
Master Ichu replied, 'Attention means attention ' —Charlotte Joku
Beck, *Nothing Special: Living Zen*

* * *

If you're in this for straightforward, practical advice on spiritual practice, you can stop now; this little Zen story tells you all you need to know. You only have any reason to read the rest of this book if any combination of the following is true:

1) Regardless of whether or not you grasp the concept of paying attention in the abstract, you need, as I did, a little help getting started.

2) Being more of a devotee than a spiritual athlete, you need some content to your attentiveness practice.

3) You'd like something more "meta" and personal than a simple list of how-to's.

4) You've heard of mindfulness practice and are intrigued, but are not ready to take the Three Refuges and become a Buddhist, and/or you are wondering if it is possible to practice mindfulness as a Christian.

5) You need help connecting the dots between contemplative practice and depression.

6) You find my convoluted reflections amusing for some reason.

If any or all of these are true, read on. Just think of me as "a householder who brings out of his storeroom new treasures as well as old." (Matthew 13:52)

Chapter 25

The Necessary Amount of Winging It

The Rev. Louis Merrill was so intellectually detached from his faith, he had so long removed himself from the necessary amount of winging it that is required of belief, that he could not accept a small but firm miracle when it happened, not only in his presence, but was even spoken by his own lips and enacted with his own hand... —John Irving, *A Prayer for Owen Meany*

* * *

The Sanskrit word *shraddha* is generally translated as "faith"—but faith has become a troublesome concept. I think this is largely due to confusion between "having faith" as an act of *trust* and having faith as an act of *belief*. The latter, with its connotations of "taking things on blind faith," is of limited usefulness in the spiritual life, and people are increasingly becoming either allergic to it—and therefore rejecting "faith" altogether as a welter of irrational superstition—or doubling down on it by clinging to received articles of faith (such as young-earth creationism, in which the earth is said to be 6,000 years old and humans are believed to have once shared it with dinosaurs) in the very teeth of reason and evidence.

Of course, the word "belief" itself can be taken in two similar ways. If I say that I "believe" in you, it could mean that I acknowledge your existence and give my intellectual assent to a certain constellation of factual statements about you. But it probably wouldn't. Yet that is precisely what people generally mean when they say they "believe" in Jesus.

Yet the belief Jesus repeatedly exhorts people to have is quite different; by "believe," Jesus means "trust." He means what I would actually mean if I said I "believed" in you: that I trust you—that I have faith in you. It doesn't mean I hold institutionally-approved opinions about your nature and origins.

For all these reasons, I prefer the way Swami Tyagananda, of the Boston Vedanta Center, characterizes the word shraddha. Rather than merely using the traditional translation, "faith," he describes shraddha as the willingness to suspend skepticism long enough to try something and see what happens. This is very much in keeping with the experimental approach that Hinduism—particularly Vedanta and Tantra—cultivates in the spiritual life. A certain amount of winging it is called for.

I exercise a lot of shraddha, in this sense, in many aspects of my spiritual life—and I urge you to do the same with this final section on spiritual practice. Unlike the old Alka Seltzer ad, I won't say, "Try it—you'll like it!" But I may say, "Try it and see what happens." It may do you good, as it has me; if it doesn't, then something else will—keep trying! It simply won't do to let the miraculous work of God go unnoticed because we, in our detachment and skepticism, are doing nothing to enhance our awareness of it.

"Taste and see that the Lord is good!" said the Psalmist. "Happy are they who put their trust in God." (Psalm 34:8)

-Chapter 26-

Two Writing Meditations[xix]

* * *

In one of my graduate music classes, our professor told us "the way to learn to write a requiem is to copy Mozart's *Requiem* by hand." There is a lot of value in the slowing-down and looking-closely that writing things out forces upon us; we can look forever at all the double-stops in the viola line, but until we've written them all out on the staff, the viola-ness of it all will never truly sink in.

Writing can also be the medium for extremely fruitful contemplative prayer. Here are two methods I have found very helpful in the past; they both opened me up to my own inner world and showed me things about myself that had been hidden.

1) Years ago, I attended a retreat at a Jesuit spiritual center with the theme Hurt and Anger. (It used to be Hurt, Anger and Guilt, one of the sisters told us, but that proved too much for one weekend.) One of the assignments we were given was to write, by hand, a dialogue between ourselves and a person toward whom we harbored unresolved anger—and to set the imagined *tête-à-tête* at the foot of the Cross of Jesus.

This exercise, pat and traditionally pious as it may sound, is extraordinarily powerful, and I have used it since when I was intractably stuck in resentment. Writing it out by hand slows the process down and forces me to really look at and think about every word, while setting the dialogue before the suffering Christ invites the Holy Spirit in as mediator, lighting up possible reasons for the other person's behavior that, in my usual chaotic mental state, had been invisible. Needless to say, it also gives a walloping dose of perspective to my complaints and grievances.

2)   In her book, *The Way of Perfection*, Saint Teresa of Avila suggests spending an hour praying the Lord's Prayer—also known as the "Our Father"—once through. I wasn't very sanguine about this one at first; it struck me—and I can't now say why—as quaint and a little mawkish. (How little I knew of the redoubtable Teresa!)

But for some reason, the idea stuck with me, emerging every now and then to nudge me toward giving it a try. Finally I gave in.

This was not presented as a writing exercise in its original form, but I decided to try it as one, since writing focuses my thoughts. I also decided to do it at the computer, rather than by hand, because I find writing by hand a chore and my handwriting is very poor, and I didn't want the process to get in the way. So I turned my attention to the prayer phrase by phrase, typing my responses as they came to me.

I was especially struck by the way fatherhood helped make the love of God real for me. So much about God's love had been pretty words, specious little nostrums that never penetrated the surface. Holding my baby girl changed all that. The past twelve years of fatherhood have been teaching me about God's love. And this late in the day, I have finally begun to see that my life is not something I have to hew out of the rock and build like a pyramid; it's not a massive DIY project complete with bootstraps for hauling oneself up by. Becoming a father has been like connecting with a huge pattern, a universal cycle, something larger than myself and all the rest of us who all travel the circuit together. Getting in touch with this pattern has been like merging into traffic or entering a skating rink; I am part of something archetypal, moving, cyclic and connected to all of humanity.

I had no idea the floodgates this exercise would open; each phrase of the prayer sparked so much in response that I have decided to include the result here as an example of what can happen. I present it mostly untouched, having only shortened it a little and edited it just enough to make it understandable.

Our Father

I am *so angry* with Clare! She and Sophie were each trying to tell me a story, and they remembered one key detail differently, and Clare's version was probably right, it made more sense, but she was absolutely determined to shout Sophie down, and I told her over and over to let Sophie tell the story her way, and then Clare could tell it in hers, but she just *defied* me and *would not stop* interrupting Sophie, just *insisting* on shouting her down; why can't Clare let someone disagree, why does she do that? I remember when I was about 10, my cousin and I had been fishing in the morning and found a little back-eddy where we caught 14 fish within a half hour or so, boom, boom, boom one right after another, and you know how on summer days when you're a kid and every moment is so full, and by the time the evening comes, the morning can seem like the day before? And my cousin was absolutely convinced that we had been fishing the day before, but he was *wrong*. I *know* he was wrong, but my big fat coarse redneck uncle said he was right and he didn't want to hear any more about it, and good God, thirty-five years later I still get angry thinking about that, what the hell is the matter with me? And I swore I would never ever do that, that everybody gets to talk and everybody gets to say it their way and nobody has the right to stifle anybody, but of course if I had defied my parents like that, I'd have gotten hit, which I will also never do, so I piped down like I was told to, but God it burns me to this day, but I wasn't telling Clare not to talk, just to let Sophie finish, why couldn't she understand that, why wouldn't she stop, why did she *defy* me like that, and why does it make me so angry, and what should I have done besides get mad and shout her down in turn, and why is it so important to her to be right, she's only six? What have I done to deserve someone so much like myself, and how can I keep her from becoming as damaged as I have become? My parents were always nagging me, nagging me, and I was a good kid—there were always so many bad things that other kids were doing and I wasn't and I never seemed to get credit for that, only nagging for the ways in which I somehow failed to measure up; dear God, please please *please* don't let me do that to my children! I was bitching about how Clare keeps grabbing food off the counter while I am cooking, and Allison said, "Don't worry, she'll grow up and leave home pretty soon;" God, I don't appreciate her enough, either.

My college roommate lost his three-year-old son to cancer, remember? (Of course You do, that's stupid.) My God—the last time I thought about that was before my own children were born; now, it's beyond my capacity to imagine, she can steal all the grated cheese she wants to; my baby is already gone, someone stole her and replaced her with a kid, and when she was three she still yelled "Daddy!"

and ran into my arms when I picked her up at daycare, and good God, if that little Daddy-adoring toddler had died, I think I'd have died with her, I'd have died for her, I'd have torn down the universe to keep it from happening, and now there's this willowy six-year-old who pisses me off so much sometimes, where did the baby I used to make laugh in the bathtub by dribbling warm water onto her belly go? Dear God, do you love me like that? Half so much?

...in Heaven, hallowed be your Name. Your kingdom come,

This I can picture, though I struggle with my tendency to imagine that it means that all the people who piss me off will just *stop it*, already; but I can imagine what it means for the unmanifested kingdom within to become manifested, for everyone to realize You and seek and serve You in all persons, loving their neighbors as themselves, though I remember what Evelyn Underhill (whose feast day is today, by the way, I don't know whether You pay attention to that sort of thing or not) said about how there is no use in our praying "thy kingdom come" every day if we are not prepared to do anything about it ourselves—got to love those no-nonsense stiff-upper-lip Greatest Generation Brits—and I don't know what I'm supposed to be doing; I don't think it means FedEx us your kingdom packed in bubble wrap, but *still...*

your will be done, on earth as in heaven.

This one, too, is relatively easy to imagine, though also difficult to divorce from my own agenda, like what Screwtape said about other people's "sins" meaning any of their actions which are annoying or inconvenient to ourselves. But I can see a world where the rich do not pick up the grapes or grain that fall to the ground, but leave them for the poor to glean, or some post-agrarian equivalent—if only all those people on the Gulf Coast could glean all that oil, I think it's a crime for BP to be selling what they reclaim, they ought to give it away. I can imagine a world without Lady Gaga in a latex nun's habit fellating a rosary, a world in which every baby is wanted from the moment of conception, a world in which no one emails Jim Wallace[20] saying "I never realized that I could be a Christian and also care about the poor," because they are taught that from the very beginning. I remember when Clare and Sophie were playing in that gazebo in the rose garden at Hershey Gardens, pretending it was their castle and the garden its grounds, and Clare said, "I'm going to give some gold to the beggars at the gate," God, I love that kid, we must be doing *something* right! (I love Sophie, too, of course, though her response was "I'm off to meet my boyfriend!"—oh God, I am so screwed.) Maybe that's where the Heaven thing comes in—when we all do Your will on the manifested plane as we all have it within us to do in unmanifested form, that will be on-earth-as-it-is-in-Heaven, Heaven being where You are, heaven-within-us now, but then us-within-heaven later, for now we see in a mirror dimly, but then face to face, right?

Give us today our daily bread

The hardest thing in the world for me—OK, one of the many hardest things in the world for me—is to trust, to

---

[20] One of the founders of the Sojourners community and editor of *Sojourners* magazine.

consider the lilies. Oh me of little faith. What was it that
Marianne Williamson said—"if a train doesn't stop at your
station, it's not your train!" But what do I do? Chase down
trains, flag them, force them to stop and take me on, then
wonder why I don't enjoy the ride, why I don't get where I
want to go. I just have to go out and get, do, make; I have
no faith at all that anything good will happen unless I am
breathing down the neck of life. And yet, every single thing
that has come to me that I wanted came when I was looking
the other way, when I wasn't chasing after it at all...Maybe
this is why everybody in every tradition emphasizes
renunciation—because only by giving up everything can we
be "as those owning nothing, yet possessing everything."
And I don't really understand the idea of Providence; why
should You give me my daily bread while others starve?
What does it mean that I have some weight to lose while
others don't have enough to eat? "Lord, forgive us that we
feast while others starve." I suppose it probably doesn't
"mean" anything except that we who have are not sharing
with those who have not—because we have no faith, we
think we have to grab all we can and hold on, and if those
people are starving it's because of their bad choices; we
make good choices, let God give them today their daily
bread. That You might do that by our hands doesn't seem
to occur to us.

Forgive us our sins as we forgive those who sin against us.

I think I can do this; I think I can finally do this.

Everybody is so scared, Lord; we hurt and reject and
devour each other because we are so afraid. When I used to
go to academic conferences, I should have realized that I
wasn't meant for that world, because I was detached enough

to look around and see how scared people are—everybody wants to seem smart, competent, good enough. We praise the emperor's clothes so much that after a while, we really see them. Forgive us. How can I cherish hatred against people who are so afraid? Thank You, thank You for allowing me to see this. My Dad said to me that he's about given up on things ever getting back to normal, but I think that things have always been a mess; maybe it's the apparatus through which we experience the world that falls apart as we get older; maybe it becomes harder to believe that we know what's right and we have the right to judge. Please, God—don't let things get back to normal; I don't want to be again that person who used to be so right while so many others were wrong. So many of the Psalms pray for a firm ground under our feet, for the Rock that is higher than I; does that prayer recur so often because You in Your mercy withhold that firm footing from which we, standing secure, are able to believe we have "arrived"? I'd rather be in transit my whole life than believe that. Never let me believe again that You created the things in others that hurt me; I know now that those things are those peoples' defences which they have erected out of fear. Hecubah was right, wailing beneath the ruined walls of Troy: "Here lies a little child, slaughtered by the Greeks because they were afraid." Forgive them; forgive me; forgive us all.

Save us from the time of trial, and deliver us from evil.

Sri Ramakrishna said that if we pour milk into water, it cannot be retrieved, while butter will float in water without being lost in it; he said that if our minds are like milk, they will be lost in the world like milk in water, whereas if they are like butter, they can float over the world without being merged in it. When I read that, I finally, this late in the day, began to understand why we bother to continue asking You to deliver us from evil, because You plainly don't, at least in the way we expect. Churn us, Lord, until we are rich enough to weather the world with integrity, until we can remain uncontaminated by it without being aloof from it, until we can be in it but not of it. You got down in the mud and breathed life into us; Jesus was born and lived an earthly life, tempted in every way as we are yet without sin. I know that we cannot escape evil, trial, temptation, testing; I no longer believe that You "deliver" us from those things by placing us in some kind of spiritual Smurf Village, with Gargamel prowling outside seeking whom he may devour. If we are not in the world, we cannot reach out the hand of love to those who are. Deliver us from forgetting who and Whose we are; let us walk through the evil of the world like Shadrach, Meshach and Abednego in the fiery furnace.

Amen.

[xix] Part of this chapter appeared under the title "A Father's Prayer (In Real Time)" in *Elephant Journal* on October 15, 2010, in a slightly different form. Used here by permission.

Chapter 27

Let Us Go and See

The Christmas story includes four different accounts of journeys, which seem, to me, to represent three distinct journey-types. The first—Mary and Joseph's journey to Bethlehem—I am calling a Journey of Necessity or Obligation.

Caesar Augustus issued a decree that a census should be taken of the entire Roman world. (This was the first census that took place while Quirinius was governor of Syria.) And everyone went to their own town to register.

So Joseph also went up from the town of Nazareth in Galilee to Judea, to Bethlehem the town of David, because he belonged to the house and line of David. He went there to register with Mary, who was pledged to be married to him and was expecting a child. While they were there, the time came for the baby to be born, and she gave birth to her firstborn, a son. She wrapped him in cloths and placed him in a manger, because there was no guest room available for them. (Luke 2:1-7, NIV)

A man and his pregnant wife travel to the man's home town to register, probably for tax purposes, at the behest of the government. Life holds many journeys of this type; among Journeys of Necessity or Obligation I would include:

- Getting an education (of one sort or another)
- Showing up for work every day (in the workplace or home)

- Rearing children
- Paying child support (when divorced or separated)
- Serving in the military (when and where it is compulsory)
- Maintaining a home
- Maintaining relationships (We may do this with joy, but it is still necessary—and it isn't always joyful, if we're honest.)
- Coping with illness or disability
- Caring for an elderly parent
- Making funeral arrangements and settling the estate when someone dies
- Serving a sentence in a correctional facility or on probation
- Undergoing rehabilitation after an injury
- Living with a non-cis/heteronormative sexual orientation or gender identity

You can probably think of a number of other examples, perhaps from your own experience or the experience of your loved ones. We all take journeys like this—metaphorical, literal, or both. We all have things we have to do, burdens we have to carry, protocols we need to observe—just on account of being human.

I call the second kind of journey I see in the Christmas story the Journey of Self-Preservation:

...an angel of the Lord appeared to Joseph in a dream. "Get up," he said, "take the child and his mother and escape to Egypt. Stay

there until I tell you, for Herod is going to search for the child to kill him."

So he got up, took the child and his mother during the night and left for Egypt, where he stayed until the death of Herod. And so was fulfilled what the Lord had said through the prophet: "Out of Egypt I called my son." (Matthew 2:13-15, NIV)

Not all of us will ever be forced to take a journey like this, but the Journey of Self-Preservation takes many forms, many of which will have touched the lives of people we know:

- Fleeing domestic and/or sexual abuse
- Entering a witness protection program
- Leaving a soul-crushing job
- Contending with potentially fatal illness or injury
- Participating in substance abuse rehabilitation, Twelve Steps, etc.
- Seeking treatment of mental illness
- Emigrating from a country at war or beset with violence and tumult

Obviously, there is a certain amount of overlap between these journeys and the Journeys of Necessity and Obligation, and neither list is exhaustive. There are things we have to do which may also keep us safe, and things we may be virtually obligated to do in order to stay safe, sane and able to discharge our other responsibilities.

Sometimes we go on what I call Journeys of Pilgrimage. These may include:

- Taking an actual religious pilgrimage to a holy site
- Going on retreat
- An adopted child's seeking his or her birth parents
- Making a journey of closure to the site of some trauma, or someplace associated with unresolved family history
- Traveling to the bedside of a sick or dying loved-one, or to a funeral (These may also, obviously, be viewed as Journeys of Obligation, depending on our feelings about the loved-one.)
- Following the Grateful Dead (which no, I never did.)

The Christmas story includes two accounts of this type of journey. Both, interestingly, involve outsiders: in the first case, it is shepherds—who were social outcasts—making the trip, and in the second it is foreigners.

There were shepherds living out in the fields nearby, keeping watch over their flocks at night. An angel of the Lord appeared to them, and the glory of the Lord shone around them, and they were terrified. But the angel said to them, "Do not be afraid. I bring you good news that will cause great joy for all the people. Today in the town of David a Savior has been born to you; he is the Messiah, the Lord. This will be a sign to you: You will find a baby wrapped in cloths and lying in a manger."

Suddenly a great company of the heavenly host appeared with the angel, praising God and saying,

Glory to God in the highest heaven, and on earth peace to those on whom his favor rests.

When the angels had left them and gone into heaven, the shepherds said to one another, "Let's go to Bethlehem and see this thing that has happened, which the Lord has told us about."

So they hurried off and found Mary and Joseph, and the baby, who was lying in the manger. When they had seen him, they spread the word concerning what had been told them about this child, and all who heard it were amazed at what the shepherds said to them. But Mary treasured up all these things and pondered them in her heart. The shepherds returned, glorifying and praising God for all the things they had heard and seen, which were just as they had been told. (Luke 2:9-15, NIV)

Of course, if an angel tells you to do something, you could argue that it is obligatory, so yes, the categories do overlap. But it is clear in context that the shepherds were eager to see the baby over Whom heaven had made such a fuss. The Magi, on the other hand, seem to have been more self-starting.

After Jesus was born in Bethlehem in Judea, during the time of King Herod, Magi from the east came to Jerusalem and asked, "Where is the one who has been born king of the Jews? We saw his star when it rose and have come to worship him." When King Herod heard this he was disturbed, and all Jerusalem with him. When he had called together all the people's chief priests and teachers of the law, he asked them where the Messiah was to be born. "In Bethlehem in Judea," they replied, "for this is what the prophet has written:

But you, Bethlehem, in the land of Judah, are by no means least among the rulers of Judah; for out of you will come a ruler who will shepherd my people Israel.

> *Then Herod called the Magi secretly and found out from them the exact time the star had appeared. He sent them to Bethlehem and said, "Go and search carefully for the child. As soon as you find him, report to me, so that I too may go and worship him."*
>
> *After they had heard the king, they went on their way, and the star they had seen when it rose went ahead of them until it stopped over the place where the child was. When they saw the star, they were overjoyed. On coming to the house, they saw the child with his mother Mary, and they bowed down and worshiped him. Then they opened their treasures and presented him with gifts of gold, frankincense and myrrh. And having been warned in a dream not to go back to Herod, they returned to their country by another route.* (Matthew 2:1-9, NIV)

In both of these Journeys of Pilgrimage, the travelers set out to seek the Promised One who had been foretold, to offer worship, adoration and gifts. But what may be less obvious is that the other two types of journeys—Obligation and Self-Preservation—are likewise fraught with opportunities for offering ourselves and our struggles to God.

I think the goal of the spiritual life is to convert all our journeys into Journeys of Pilgrimage. If we are obligated to do something, we can "make a virtue of necessity," as the saying goes, and do it in a spirit of service. "If anyone wants to sue you and take your shirt, hand over your coat as well. If anyone forces you to go one mile, go with them two miles." (Matthew 5:40-41) If we are serious about "seeking and serving Christ in all persons, loving your neighbor as yourself," we can find ways to make a loving offering of what life obliges us to do.

If we are fleeing the floodwaters to get our children to higher ground, or leaving a dangerous area to increase their measure of safety, or getting out of an abusive relationship, it may not be necessary to remind ourselves that everything we have, including our very lives, is held on trust for God and worth preserving if only for that reason; the drive to keep our loved ones secure, and ourselves alive for their sake as well as our own, already has a sacred character. If we manage to notice and acknowledge that fact, our Journeys of Necessity can become Journeys of Pilgrimage.

The heroes of myth rarely undertake their heroic quests out of sheer wanderlust or high spirits; most often, they are driven to them by dire necessity; for the preservation of their own lives, and out of obligation to the well-being of their people, the hero undertakes the journey of pilgrimage from which, if all goes to plan, he or she will return victorious and forever changed. As Joseph Campbell described it in *The Hero with a Thousand Faces*,

A hero ventures forth from the world of common day into a region of supernatural wonder: fabulous forces are there encountered and a decisive victory is won: the hero comes back from this mysterious adventure with the power to bestow boons on his fellow man. (Campbell 23)

For me—and, I suspect, for many readers of this book—it was depression that forced me to undertake my Journey of Pilgrimage, to discover who I really was, what I really loved, and what I was really meant to be doing. It was a Journey of Necessity and Obligation, insofar as I wanted to stay married, and a Journey of Self-Preservation to the extent that I didn't want to waste my life being miserable. But no matter what external forces drive us to undertake our life journeys, if we can tackle them in this spirit of pilgrimage, we need be neither conscripts nor victims, but pilgrims and, perhaps, heroes.

-*Chapter 28*-

Why I Clean the Bacon Pans (A Vegetarian's Shrove Tuesday Tantra)[xx]

What God has made clean, do not call unclean. —Acts 10:15

* * *

I used to have a job in a Catholic Charities group home, much of which involved changing the soiled sheets and menstrual pads of severely mentally challenged young women. At the time, I didn't realize what an opportunity for spiritual growth I was experiencing. Cutting my children's umbilical cords, changing their diapers, giving Communion to a woman hours before her death, laying hands on the dying and praying with them, dabbling consecrated wine on the lips of the comatose, baptizing a tiny newborn with his intestines wrapped up in a plastic bag on the bed next to him—these have constituted many of the most profoundly "spiritual" moments of my life. And if I ran the zoo, Andres Serrano's infamous *Piss Christ* photograph— featuring a plastic crucifix submerged in the photographer's blood and urine—would hang in the break room of every Christian group home, hospital and hospice, because it is in the blood and sewage that we find Jesus.

Some of these activities were professional, while others (including many I have not mentioned) were done on a volunteer basis. It is a commonplace that helping others can lift one out of depression, and I have found it true in my own experience. Participating in a march for justice, helping in a homeless shelter, volunteering through a place of worship or community center—besides taking us out of ourselves, they give us reason to feel good about the way we spend our time and effort, both while we are doing it and for some time after. (And if the yogis are right, *seva,* or selfless service, "burns the seeds" of accrued karma, which can't be bad.)

And I think there is, if not a greater value, at least a unique value in service one finds personally distasteful. The great French mystic Brother Lawrence of the Resurrection spent most of the cloistered part of his life working in the monastery kitchen, a job he especially disliked. And one of St. Francis of Assisi's first acts after his conversion was kissing a leper—a class of people for whom he'd always had a particular horror and disgust.

In a way, one could regard Francis's kiss as a Tantric purging of desire and aversion. The much-misunderstood classical Christian ascetic discipline known as the "mortification of the flesh" has the same aim as much Tantric practice: to free the self of the bonds of desire and aversion.

In his commentary on the *Tantraloka,* one of the central texts of Tantric thought, Jayaratha (1150-1200 CE) explains that would-be initiates into Tantra of the Kashmir Shaivites (devotees of Shiva) must use objects and ingest substances "detested by people, prohibited by the sacred texts, disgusting and despised." Those who wish to enter the Kashmiri Tantra must become familiar, even comfortable, with what is "inauspicious and illicit." (Dupuche 132) Squeamishness won't cut it.

The Kashmiri Tantra used these extreme methods for two reasons: 1) to transgress religious boundaries and mores in order to transcend them and 2) to wean aspirants away from the duality of attraction and repulsion.

"[P]ractitioners (who) wish to express and develop the non-dual state...which does not oppose pleasure and horror...make use of both pleasure and horror and by these means show that they transcend all dualism." (Dupuche 67)[21]

The further one progressed in the mysteries of the Kashmiri Tantra, the more one transgressed every imaginable social and religious boundary. If the aspirants made it as far as the *kula* ceremony, they would drink from a cup containing a dozen items, all of them repellant to Hindus, and many of them repellant to everybody: wine, semen, urine, menstrual blood, feces, phlegm, human flesh, beef, goat meat, fish, fowl, onion and garlic. (Dupuche 70) The last two are considered "brain poison for meditators," but no one can convince me that Francis of Assisi, Teresa of Avila, St. John of the Cross, Catherine of Genoa and Brother Lawrence didn't eat plenty of garlic. But garlic aside, it is hard to imagine a more daunting exercise in sublimating the sense of aversion in the name of equanimity, non-dualism and non-attachment.

When male initiates took part in the *maithuna* ceremony— the ritual sexual intercourse that is the basis for the "Tantric sex" which is about all the West knows, or thinks it knows, about Tantra—Abhinavagupta (c.950-1020 CE) recommended in the *Tantraloka* that they perform the act with adulterous women, whose "husbands are an out-caste, a black, an archer, a butcher, a tanner, a eunuch, a fisherman, a potter"—those on the lowest rungs of the Hindu social ladder. The Kashmiri Shaivites "attach no

---

[21] These extremes are more typical of the so-called "Left Hand" school of Tantric thought; "Right Hand" Tantra emphasizes more orthodox techniques, such as meditation.

importance to classes and conditions but on the contrary take pleasure in befriending the wretched and the dishonest." (Dupuche)

As a Christian, I respect that.

While Jesus was having dinner at Matthew's house, many tax collectors and sinners came and ate with him and his disciples. When the Pharisees saw this, they asked his disciples, "Why does your teacher eat with tax collectors and sinners?" On hearing this, Jesus said, "It is not the healthy who need a doctor, but the sick. But go and learn what this means: 'I desire mercy, not sacrifice.' For I have not come to call the righteous, but sinners." (Matthew 9:10-17, NIV)

I thought of this passage when I read, in *Autobiography of a Yogi,* Swami Yogananda's account of his first meeting with Swami Dayananda, who explained that he had taken neither food nor drink during the preceding four days of travel because "I never eat on trains, filled with the heterogeneous vibrations of worldly people." Of course, if one believes the vibrations emitted by the stars and planets affect us spiritually—this belief being the basis of Hindu astrology—it makes sense that the vibrations emitted by spiritually heedless human beings in an enclosed space would also take their toll.

To the notion that other people's worldly vibes might get into one's food and give one spiritual cooties, Jesus might have answered, "What goes into someone's mouth does not defile them, but what comes out of their mouth, that is what defiles them." (Matthew 15:11)

Ever since the Apostolic Era—when Jesus' first disciples were still alive—Christian doctrine has held that all foods are clean. "If you enter a town and it welcomes you,"

Jesus told his disciples, "eat whatever is set before you" without any scruples based in Jewish dietary law. (Luke 10:18) Whether dealing with forbidden foods, social outcastes (foreigners and tax collectors), or physical illness of a type that would defile a Jewish man who came in contact with it (lepers and the woman with vaginal bleeding,) Jesus, like a good Tantrika, is "the one who does not recoil from anything." (Dupuche 133)

So while vegetarianism is not unheard-of among Christians—the Trappist monks have been vegetarians since the 17th century, as were the desert hermits of the Roman era—it is not exactly mainstream.

I've been a vegetarian since 1987—a little more that half my lifetime ago. I have neither knowingly cooked nor eaten meat in all that time. This is unusual for a Christian, and I have taken some heat for it from Christians more conservative than myself, who claim, essentially, that my vegetarianism reintroduces squeamishness into an area to which Jesus Himself had given the all-clear.

At my Episcopalian parish (where nobody judges my vegetarianism so far as I know) bacon holds a position just slightly below Holy Communion, and its great Feast Day is Shrove Tuesday, when it shares the spotlight with live Dixieland Jazz, sausage, coffee, Mardi Gras beads and, of course, mountains of pancakes. In our parish, this annual pre-Lenten blowout is a fundraiser in support of the youth Sunday school's pilgrimage to Pine Ridge, South Dakota, and as one of their teachers, I roll up my sleeves and pitch in to help out. Long before the hungry parishioners pour into the hall to drop money in the baskets and load their plates with sweet, fatty, festive food, I station myself by the big double sink to wash the baking trays the bacon is cooked on, preparing them for the next batch in the production line of sizzling pork belly.

I've been a vegetarian so long that I avert my eyes when passing the butcher's counter in the grocery store; as a child, I'd have seen food behind the glass, but now I only see dead flesh. So twice a year (we also bacon-out on our parish patron St. Martin's feast day) I set myself the little Christian Tantric spiritual exercise of rolling up my sleeves and washing seared pig bits off a bunch of baking pans, and going home smelling like hickory smoked lard. Of course it's a small thing, and mostly symbolic; I've done it often enough by this point that I scarcely have any aversion left to overcome. But we have to take our spiritual vitamins on the run; even if we had more time for formal spiritual practice, we probably wouldn't use it, and if you spend a lot of time in the kitchen, the kitchen is as good a place as any to practice in. St. Teresa of Avila put it this way:

Don't think that if you had a great deal of time you would spend more of it in prayer. Get rid of that idea! God gives more in a moment than in a long period of time, for His actions are not measured by time at all. Know that even when you are in the kitchen, Our Lord is moving among the pots and pans.

[xx] "Why I Clean the Bacon Pans: A Vegetarian's Shrove Tuesday Tantra" first appeared in *Elephant Journal* on February 19, 2015, in a slightly different form. Used here by permission.

-Chapter 29-

The Butterfly House[xxi]

The world you see has nothing to do with reality. It is of your own making, and it does not exist. —A Course in Miracles, Lesson 14

* * *

The butterflies no longer flock to my daughter.

When Clare was four, her daycare center hatched some butterflies in a small screen tent. On the day they released them, I came to pick Clare up on the playground and saw her standing very still with an ear-to-ear grin and a half-dozen butterflies all over herself. "They just went to her," her teachers said. The same thing happened whenever we visited a butterfly house: without any particular effort on her part, Clare would attract *Lepidoptera* like she exuded nectar; we'd have to check her for stowaways before leaving.

Within a couple years, it didn't happen any more. Maybe some essence of baby innocence that once rose up from her no longer wafted from the self-conscious first-grader she had become. She tried, and my heart ached as I watched her patiently holding out a finger to the unresponsive insects, taut with wanting and, ultimately, deflated with disappointment.

That disappointment colored the whole butterfly house experience for a long time. For years, before soccer and lacrosse and circus classes and standardized tests took us away from public gardens and museums, she still made a beeline for the butterfly house wherever there was one, but a veil of wishing and remembering arose between her and her surroundings. A part of the Garden was lost, and that loss imparted its flavor to what remained.

We experience, not the world around us, but our thoughts and feelings about that world. How can we get out of ourselves enough to actually experience our lives, unfiltered by shoulds, oughts and if-onlys?

There is a yoga discipline called *pratyahara*, which means "withdrawal of the senses." During practice, the mind is supposed to be so focused that no distractions are able to enter our awareness. And that withdrawal is a good thing—I want to experience my experiences fully. But I like to think of pratyahara more broadly than that. When I am on a hike or picnic or retreat, for instance, I don't want radio, television, recorded music or the internet intruding; I want to withdraw my senses from the overstimulating media that usually occupy them, so that my mind may be more available to the subtler experiences around me.

But even then, my "monkey mind," as the Buddhists call it, continues to interpose itself between my awareness and the world. Everything I see and hear reminds me of something I need to do, someone who is trying my patience, another time and place in which I saw or heard something similar, something I know, or wish I knew, about the thing seen or heard. Nothing just is what it is on its own terms—everything becomes an object of my judgment and analysis, a springboard for my daydreams.

So I find it useful to regularly withdraw my attention, not from external stimuli, but from my internal commentary on them, which allows things to be more what they are. Be a stranger—be "not from around here," the better to experience things as for the first time. It helps if the field of stimuli is relatively narrow—any activity I do more or less mechanically can clear a space for contemplative practice—and on a good day, when I am mowing the lawn or cleaning up the kitchen or folding laundry, I will remember to take advantage of the opportunity. Here's what I do:

I begin by becoming aware of my breathing, which takes my attention away from my thoughts. The moment I begin this is one of the most satisfying moments of the day; there is a sense of release and restfulness, but not a somnolent restfulness—rather, a heightened awareness charged with energy even as it calms me, that gives me a pale glimpse of what it means to be "he who in the midst of the greatest silence and solitude finds the intensest activity, and in the midst of the intensest activity, the silence and solitude of the desert." (Vivekananda, Karma Yoga 11)

I then begin to pray my mantra. I use the so-called Jesus Prayer: *Lord Jesus Christ, Son of God, have mercy on me.* This prayer, adapted from the words of the blind beggar Bartimaeus, who called out to Jesus from the roadside (Mark 10:46-52), has been used in contemplative practice since the Desert Fathers and Mothers, and is still widely practiced in the Eastern churches

(A word of explanation: the Greek word *eleos*, which is translated "mercy," actually has a broader meaning than we ordinarily ascribe to it, including not only forgiveness but healing. The word has the same root as *elia*, meaning "olive," because prayer for healing was—as it often still is—accompanied by anointing with [olive] oil. The point being that a repeated prayer for mercy is not necessarily the grimly penitential exercise it might sound like.)

Now here's the counter-intuitive part: "*When we repeat the mantram, we are not hypnotizing ourselves, or woolgathering, or turning our back on the world.*" (Easwaran 6)

You'd think that repeating something over and over in your head would just add to the chaos, but in fact it does just the opposite. When the "monkey mind" is occupied with the mantra, I am actually freed from the distraction of memory, anticipation, plans, regrets, fantasies and all the other busywork that occupies me most of the time. So I am able to see, hear, feel everything much more vividly, without a layer of commentary between my deeper self and my experience. What a potato feels like as I rub the dirt off its surface under the tap, how the ocean sounds on the far side of a stand of trees through which the wind is blowing, the licorice smell of a pile of pulled weeds—everything is novel and intensified, unfiltered by commentary and classification. Experience bypasses the monkey mind and registers more directly.

This is how I think of the practice of mindfulness: I walk out of my head, and into my skin; out of the swirl of memory and anticipation of which my thoughts usually consist, and into the here and now of where I actually am and what I'm actually doing. Out of the dream, and into wakefulness—at least for a short time.

The transition isn't instantaneous; generally, there's a brief intervening period between walking down the sidewalk by myself, or ambling through the woods with my dogs, entirely absorbed in my inner drama, and coming to a full awareness of the moment. When I remember to do it, I allow my mantra to start spinning slowly in the back of my head—it reminds me of those rotating rock tumblers, sometimes—and the part of my brain generating memory, anticipation and fantasy becomes reassigned to the new task of keeping the mantra going. Soon I am noticing things that, even on the most familiar walks, I hadn't noticed before, sensing the air on my skin and the ground under my feet, and feeling my shoulders relax as my face turns from the ground to the world around me.

But for just a few seconds between the time when I am walking around surrounded by a cloud of my own thoughts like Pig Pen in his billowing dust cloud, and the time during which I walk as a more-or-(much)-less enlightened Bodhisattva, free of craving, aversion and suffering, the landscape around me teems with memories. In the woods, I see smaller versions of my children running ahead, shouting, splashing in the stream; on the sidewalk, I see them in the big double stroller I pushed over endless miles; looking out over the snowy fields of Lebanon County, I see my young wife-to-be with a big, wet snowball running down her hair and murder in her eye. But if I persevere, the memories fade into the background and the actual here-and-now becomes available to me, and I to it.

The Indian sage Patanjali wrote, "The Seer is intelligence only, and though pure, sees through the coloring of the intellect." (Vivekananda, *Raja Yoga* 143) When the intellect is otherwise occupied, the view is less colored. The monkey mind leaves you alone. Think of it this way: there was once a Jewish village that was being tormented by a demon, so the people set up a greased pole outside the village and challenged the demon to climb it—which kept the demon occupied and allowed the villagers to get on with their lives. The prayer is like that greased pole. If you've ever sat your children down in front of a video to get them out of your hair (not that you or I would ever do that) you know what I mean.

If you have never thought of your mind as having multiple constituencies, you may be scratching your head now, but the idea is actually very old and widespread. Generally, the distinction is made between the unchanging, eternal inner Self—of which we are mostly or entirely unaware—and the morass of thoughts and emotions with which we usually identify ourselves, but which are not actually *us*. In contemplation, we can realize that, and be as unperturbed by our inner dramas as the mountain is by the weather.

(Cautionary note: don't get the impression that I spend a lot of time in that state. "How rare the moment, and how brief its duration!" said John of the Cross—and he was pretty good. Better than me.)

This undifferentiated awareness that Patanjali called the "Seer"—called in Sanskrit the *purusha*—is, in yogic thought, the seat of the true Self, and is unchanging and eternal, despite the apparent "coloring" imparted to it by the intellect. The Bible similarly distinguishes between the *psyche,* or "soul" (Hebrew *nephesh)*—which is unique to the individual—and the *pneuma,* or "spirit," (Hebrew *ruach)* which comes from God.

The belief that "spirit" is of God is behind the doctrine of the "Body of Christ" being made up, collectively, of all the faithful. "Christ has no body now on earth but yours," wrote Teresa of Avila; "no hands, not feet on earth but yours. Yours are the eyes through which He looks compassion on this world." Through our perishable eyes, something eternal looks out. So when we get our transient "weather" selves out of the way, our eternal "mountain" selves are made available to God—even identified with God. "I live," said Paul, "now not I, but Christ lives within me." (Galatians 2:20) The divine spark within each soul, which in Sanskrit it called the Atman, is identical to the Transcendent Absolute, or Brahman.

Which is why I'm glad my children are at a Friends school. The Quaker doctrine of the Inner Light—the belief that "there is that of God in everyone"—is so much in keeping with the baptismal vow to "seek and serve Christ in all persons, loving your neighbor as yourself." Western Christians—notably the 14th-century German mystic Meister Eckhardt—have said before that we all have a divine spark within us, and been suppressed for it—but thanks be to God and William Penn, the notion has at last taken root and flourished.

This is why Quaker worship is so contemplative. Everyone assembles and sits in silence. If someone is "moved" to speak, they do. At weekly Meeting for Worship at our girls' school, the whole period (only twenty minutes, since even the kindergarteners are included) usually passes in total silence. The practice being cultivated is a clarifying of the inner faculties and a patient waiting for the promptings of the Spirit—the illumination of the Inner Light. If we are to hear the still, small voice, we need to be still ourselves. We think that sleep is quiet and wakefulness active, but the opposite is the case: our busy, buzzy brains are keeping us asleep and shutting out the light; when they become quiet, the light dawns and we can awaken and see.

When I awake, I shall be satisfied, beholding Your face. (Psalm 17:15)

One evening, while walking up Nicollet Avenue to my apartment in Minneapolis, I heard an African American man's voice behind me sigh heavily—"What a day, what a day!" he said. That sounded like an invitation to talk, so I turned around and introduced myself, and we walked together up the main street of that part of the city—a street I thought I knew, but realized as we walked that I didn't. As I, a white graduate student in classical music, walked with this black working man, I almost literally saw a whole different street around us, one I had never seen before.

People I had never previously noticed greeted us—black people, Lakotas, urban working people, people who must have been there before but who had never registered on my consciousness. My frame of reference had not included them—but my companion's frame, which I was temporarily sharing, did. I ended up walking about a mile past my street, so fascinating was the experience. I grew up some during that walk.

"When I was a child" wrote Paul, "I spoke like a child, thought like a child, and reasoned like a child. When I became a man, I gave up my childish ways." (1 Corinthians 13:11) One sure sign of spiritual maturity, it seems to me, is that we no longer let what we want to be experiencing prevent us from enjoying what we actually are experiencing.

I knew that Clare would get over her disappointment about the butterflies. Sooner or later, I was sure, she will stop wanting so badly for them to come back, and then one of two things would happen: 1) they *would* come back, because her desire was no longer driving them away. (If you doubt that this happens, try to remember the process of finding a prom date; is anything more off-putting than a desperate desire to be asked? The whole universe works this way, I'm sure of it.) Or, 2) she would be happy to view the butterflies where they were. (I didn't reckon, at the time, on the third possibility—that she would become too busy to hang around butterfly houses with her Dad any more.) In any case, I knew her wishes for the future and memories of the past would no longer contaminate her experience in the present. I hope and pray that this will prove true in other areas of her life as she grows up.

I used to have trouble reconciling Paul's words about "childish ways" with the words of Jesus: "I tell you with certainty: unless you change and become like little

children, you will never enter the kingdom of heaven."
(Matthew 18:3) How can we become like little children and,
at the same time, give up childish ways? I remember driving
Clare to a birthday party—she was five at the time—and
trying to explain to her why some of the drivers around us
were so aggressive and unsafe. "Sometimes the world isn't
a very nice place," I told her. After a long silence, she said,
"But Daddy, the world is still very pretty." In that moment,
I blessed God and knew that Jesus was right. Why on earth
are we to put that childish vision behind us?

But I think I've worked it out. (Don't thank me yet;
there'll be plenty of time for that later and besides, there
are probably 800 spiritual classics I haven't read yet that
already say this.) I think it breaks down like this:

1)   As infants, we are undifferentiated from our
        parents, our world, and God. We are
        unselfconscious. We are totally dependent,
        and all our needs are met. Everything is new
        and astonishing to us. We experience our
        surroundings with great immediacy. Good
        and evil have no meaning. The mythic
        analog is the Garden of Eden; my butterfly-
        spangled daughter still had one foot there.

2)   As we grow, we individuate and differentiate
        ourselves as we become self-conscious. As
        we grow in experience, our world loses its
        newness, and we begin to classify things,
        viewing everything through the lens of what
        we remember and anticipate. We must
        increasingly meet our own needs. We have
        eaten the fruit of the Tree of the Knowledge

of Good and Evil and been expelled from the Garden. The medieval world reckoned this as happening around the age of seven, when, having reached full verbal competence and the Church's "age of accountability," the child was considered morally responsible. (Postman) The mythic analog is the Fall; I believe my daughter was undergoing it as the butterflies deserted her.

3)   When we are able to see things as they are rather than as our distorting desires make them appear, we reunite with God on an adult level, combining the trust and boundarylessness of infancy with the (relative) wisdom of adulthood. We are "born again." Communion—when "we who are many are one body, for we all share in the one bread"—is the outward invocation of this state; mythically, it is represented by the New Heaven and New Earth of the Book of Revelation 21.

And that's something to hope for: the veils drop away, and we no longer have a chattering monkey-mind full of judging and desire between our inner selves and creation— no longer have to view the heavens through the distorting turmoil of emotional and intellectual "weather." Even if heaven and earth aren't actually new then, they will be new to us, because we will experience them for the first time. And if Paul is right, while we struggle to pierce the veil, we can be sure that it obscures the view only in one direction; though we struggle to know God, God already knows us:

Now we see in a mirror dimly, but then face to face; now I know in part, but then I will know fully just as I also have been fully known. (1 Corinthians 13:12, ESV)

---

xxi "The Butterfly House" first appeared in *Elephant Journal* under the title "Seeing the World as It Is" on March 8, 2011, in a slightly different form. Used here by permission.

-Chapter 30-

Impure Spirits[xxii]

When an impure spirit comes out of a person, it goes through arid places seeking rest and does not find it. Then it says, 'I will return to the house I left.' When it arrives, it finds the house unoccupied, swept clean and put in order. Then it goes and takes with it seven other spirits more wicked than itself, and they go in and live there. And the final condition of that person is worse than the first. –Matthew 12:43-45, NLT

* * *

There are a lot of books out there peddling tools and techniques for coping with depression. Many of them promise to teach you how to use Zen, or Yoga, or prayer, or exercise or any of a number of other things to help get you off your anti-depressant medication. Being medication-free is presented as the goal—the clear implication being that dependence on medication is undesirable.

I have nothing to say about the claims these writers make that their techniques can alleviate depression. I daresay many of them can—though I suspect it is may be faith and investment in these techniques, rather than the techniques themselves, that do the trick. "If you truly believe that you can relieve your depression by standing on your head and spitting nickels for an hour every afternoon, it is likely that this incommodious activity will do you tremendous good." (Solomon 123)

But about the claim, explicit or implied, that you ought to be able to cope without medication, and that you are somehow a failure if you are not, I have this to say, and say emphatically: *Don't let anyone bully, shame or manipulate you into coping with your depression in what they think is the one and only right way.*

Claims about the deleterious effects of medication are not supported by science—especially when compared with the effects of recurrent depression. Notwithstanding that there is "no evidence of negative effects of long-term medication," people assume that your ultimate goal is to be drug free, even at the risk of recurring illness. "(W)ellness is still…associated not with achieving control of your problem, but with discontinuation of medication." (Solomon, "Anatomy of Melancholy")

The fact is, the more often you relapse into depression, the worse off you are, because each time the disease returns it can do irreversible damage. Except under the close supervision of a psychiatrist, the common approach of going off your meds when you feel better in order to "see what happens" is an invitation to sickness that may leave you worse off than before, and less able to benefit from the drugs whose use you have discontinued, not for medically valid reasons, but because society makes us feel as though we ought to be able to get along without them.

"If you stimulate seizures in an animal every day," says Andrew Solomon, "the seizures become automatic: the animal will go on having them even if you withdraw the stimulation. Similarly, a brain that has gone into depression several times may return to depression. Brain-imaging scans have indicated that depression changes both the structure and the biochemistry of the brain. Medication-responsive patients may cease to respond over the long term if they cycle on and off the medications; with each episode, there is a ten percent increase in the risk that the depression will become chronic." (Solomon, "Anatomy of Melancholy")

Once the evil spirit has been driven out, Jesus said, the formerly-possessed is at risk for a relapse on a larger scale; without a security system in place to guard the newly-swept house from re-invasion, the last state of the victim will be worse than the first.

This leads us to another important point: once the "demon" of depression is kicked to the curb, it is important to put something else in its place before it comes back and brings its friends. Therapy, a behavioral plan and an exercise regimen—both physical and spiritual—can hang a "no vacancy" sign that, along with medication, can safeguard against a relapse.

This can be counter-intuitive during the period when anti-depressants are kicking in, and the patient is looking better on the outside; it's tempting, when seeing the clouds start to lift as medication takes effect, to think, "We're done!", and neglect the other safeguards.

For someone who suffers from moderate to severe depression, the point when medications start making a difference is a time to watch. Normally, you'd think, "That's great! His medications are kicking in, and things are going to get better." But things aren't in sync yet, and this can be a dangerous period. Depression saps energy to such an extent that even if someone wants to commit suicide, he may not be able to summon up the energy to do it. Medications will help to lift the depression, but they tend to work in stages. They tend to affect energy first, mood second, so she will get back her energy before *her mood changes, and that puts her at risk. For those first few days or weeks, she may still want to commit suicide, and now she has the energy to act.* (Strauss 115)

I hasten to add that it's important not to overstate the danger of anti-depressants. A 2007 meta-analysis of the effects of anti-depressants on children and adolescents with pediatric major depressive disorder, obsessive-compulsive disorder, and anxiety disorders found a two-fold increase in suicidal ideation among its subjects; (Bridge) some of the studies analyzed were widely trumpeted in the popular press, and many people are aware of them. However, it is important to bear in mind that that twofold increase meant a leap from 2% to 4% of patients having suicidal thoughts—and none of the patients in any of the studies actually committed suicide. In any case, forewarned is forearmed: we now know that behavioral and therapeutic strategies need to be in place along with anti-depressant treatment in order for the treatment to be fully effective. If the only thing that changes is the patient's ability to function, the demon may return virtually unopposed.

Unfortunately, many of us, when we feel the malaise returning, do exactly the opposite of what needs to be done. When the demon is at the door, instead of remaining faithful to our personal sadhanas, we back away from them; we haven't got the energy, we tell ourselves, or we just need to get some "real" work done in order to feel better. I think this is why so many legends of demons and vampires insist that these creatures cannot enter our homes unless we invite them in—and why they are portrayed as consummately skillful in persuading us to do just that.

According to legend, the altar in the Jerusalem Temple concealed a shaft that led all the way down into the Primal Abyss. When the primordial chaos bubbled up through the shaft periodically and threatened to engulf the world, the high priest would write the Tetragrammaton— the four-letter Unpronounceable Name of God—onto a pottery shard and drop it down the shaft. The chaos would then subside.

My spiritual and behavioral practices are my personal Tetragrammaton against the threatening chaos— but I usually do more or less the opposite of what the high priest did. When my inner abyss of negative thoughts, rumination and despondency begins to bubble up, I stow the shards and bury the brush, instead fighting the chaos with the very things of which it is made: frantic efforting, dispersed energies, guilt, shame and "the conscious fret and fume of resolutions and clenched teeth." (Lewis 28) Like the woodsman in Stephen Covey's *Seven Habits*, I exhaust myself trying to cut down a tree with a dull saw, because I'm too busy to stop and sharpen the saw.

When an occasional eruption sends up a flood of bubbling chaos, I back off from doing the very things that keep it at bay. I become much too "busy" for *asana* practice, meditation, prayer, study, or healthy eating and sleeping. And of course, the more I neglect those things, the less able I am to accomplish the tasks that somehow seem more urgent.

I end up physically debilitated and emotionally depressed. Nothing seems meaningful or worth the effort, and the very sky overhead feels like a suffocating leaden

dome. I understand why Sylvia Plath likened her episodes
of depression to a bell jar coming down over her.

When I found myself, after an early relapse, sitting
in a coffee shop, trying to write an article while hunched
over my laptop like Snoopy pretending to be a vulture
because my back was painfully seized up, with a whole
autumn's worth of unraked leaves in the back yard and a
house cluttered enough to get lost in, I finally woke up and
realized that trying to stuff the chaos back down the shaft
on my own wasn't working any better this time than it had
the previous times. I had gone off my medication because I
felt better, and the demon had come back with a posse.
Slowly, with the help of a loving spouse, medical
intervention, and a renewed sadhana, I began to reclaim my
house.

The challenge, of course, is to remember to do what
is necessary for well-being when the mind is telling you to
put those things on hold. *You don't have time to sharpen that
saw,* the mind will tell you—*keep sawing, because this tree needs to
come down right now!* But of course, it is precisely when you
think you have more urgent things to attend to than your
spiritual practice becomes so vitally important. I imagine
that's why, even when "many were coming and going" till
He "had no time even to eat," Jesus still made time to
"withdraw into a lonely place" to pray. (Mark 6:31) Gandhi
said that he meditated for an hour every day, except on
particularly busy days, when he meditated for two hours.

Sometimes it's just a question of getting started—
taking the first step. Small adjustments in behavior,
practice, or even environment can generate the momentum
that propels us to larger changes.

It could be in his surroundings. Redecorate by picking up one new pillow, one new throw, moving the furniture, putting up a new picture, different napkins...These small changes...are easy to institute, they offer choices, and they make her feel she has some control over what happens. But the most important thing they do is make her environment—what she experiences with her senses—feel different. (Strauss 106)

My home office is a mirror of my state of mind; the messier it is, the more mental malaise it is reflecting. But it also causes that which it reflects, like the Queen's magic mirror in Snow White: it reinforces in me that which it reports to me. So changing the environment can help change the mental state the environment has been reflecting; it works both ways.

I once began the process of lifting off the bell jar by simply getting my frame drums[22] off the floor of my office and hanging them on the wall. Having done that, I was inspired to get my diplomas out of their drawer, frame them, and mount them on the walls. A couple of lovely prints followed. By this time, I was inspired enough to completely clean out and reorganize my office—and the better it looked, the better I felt. I have kept it neat and organized ever since, and it does great things for my mood state. Mirrors like that, it turns out, are two-way.

The clean office, the anti-depressant medication, the meditation practice, the physical exercise: these are the new tenants in my house that are filling up the space that could otherwise be claimed by the demon and his seven friends. There is an Indian saying that just as one uses one thorn to remove another thorn stuck in the foot or finger, so we can use good thoughts to drive out bad ones.

---

[22] Any drums that are wider than they are deep, like tambourines.

If you know anyone who practices the Twelve Steps, you may have noticed that many "friends of Bill" allow new, relatively benign addictions to take the place of the addiction that was killing them. I have a recovering alcoholic friend who is now the most voracious caffeine freak I have ever known—and good on him, because the booze was ruining his life. I know a number of recovering alcoholics who took up smoking in recovery; yes, they tell me, smoking may kill me in the long run, but drinking could kill me tomorrow. Anne Lamott has said that getting all one's addictions under control at once is like putting an octopus to bed—but if you know that a helpful, or at least less harmful, tentacle can keep a malevolent one from strangling you, then by all means, favor that tentacle. Whatever it takes to keep the demon and his crew from re-occupying your house, that is what you need to be doing— whatever the peddlers of a "medication-free lifestyle" may try to sell you.

---

xxii A portion of this chapter appeared under the title "Alka-Seltzer for the Primal Abyss" on *Elephant Journal* on December 14, 2010, in a slightly different form. Used here by permission.

Chapter 31

Always Be Ready to Be Surprised

In the beginner's mind there are many possibilities, but in the expert's mind there are few. –Shunryu Suzuki, *Zen Mind, Beginner's Mind*

* * *

I know a great many things about myself, and most of them are wrong.

Life with depression is a constricted life, with options pared back and elbow room at a premium. Everything we think we know hardens and sets until new possibilities cannot break through. The voices in our heads chant a litany of failure and debility until we believe we have tried everything, and none of it works.

For instance, for years I believed that I just don't "get anything out of" guided visualization. I figured I respond better to sounds, I lack imagination and attention span for the visual, I'm not a narrative thinker, yadda yadda yadda. I was very sure of all this; I had "been there and done that." Then, during my training at the Shalem Institute for Spiritual Formation, I experienced a guided meditation on a gospel story often known as The Woman with the Flow of Blood:

(A) woman was there who had been subject to bleeding for twelve years. She had suffered a great deal under the care of many doctors and had spent all she had, yet instead of getting better she grew worse. When she heard about Jesus, she came up behind him in the crowd and touched his cloak, because she thought, "If I just touch his clothes, I will be

healed." Immediately her bleeding stopped and she felt in her body that she was freed from her suffering. At once Jesus realized that power had gone out from him. He turned around in the crowd and asked, "Who touched my clothes?" "You see the people crowding against you," his disciples answered, "and yet you can ask, 'Who touched me?' "But Jesus kept looking around to see who had done it. Then the woman, knowing what had happened to her, came and fell at his feet and, trembling with fear, told him the whole truth. He said to her, "Daughter, your faith has healed you. Go in peace and be freed from your suffering. (Mark 5:25-34, NIV)

The guide simply read the story twice, very slowly, then instructed me to imagine, in as much detail as possible, that I was witnessing the event myself. She didn't fill in any specifics, which gave my mind the opportunity it needed to go off on one of its bizarre flights.

I found myself picturing the story taking place, for some reason, in a Pennsylvania Dutch country market—a setting with which I am very familiar. I could see the bins of big belt buckles, banjos and mandolins hanging on a rack, baskets of kitchen implements, tables of pies, rack upon rack of Christian books and bin after bin of fresh produce. Amish and Mennonite men and women were all around me, as well as their more "worldly" neighbors who, while not officially "plain," were certainly not "fancy." I smelled freshly ground horseradish, heard snatches of conversation in Pennsilfaanisch, and breathed in the atmosphere of religious conservatism and rural tradition.

As a group of men came in one of the side doors, a palpable current of hostility began to flow from the people around me toward the man at the group's center. *Who does he think he is? He grew up right around here like the rest of us; where does he get off acting like some kind of leader? Where did he get all this so-called wisdom from?* Though many seemed to welcome the man's arrival, others obviously thought him far above himself.

But the animosity toward Jesus was nothing compared to the all-but-tangible hatred toward the woman who crept fearfully up to touch one of his Muckmaster® boots. *What does she think she's doing? It may not be her fault, but the Law is the Law. She must have done **something** wrong or this wouldn't have happened to her.*

Now, one thing that may escape modern readers is that in Jesus' time, a woman with a "flow of blood"—that is, vaginal bleeding—would have been considered "unclean" under Jewish law, and any man she touched would then be considered unclean also. This accounts for the fearful way in which the woman approached Jesus—who, never one to prioritize the letter of the law over its spirit—healed and blessed her. When the people around me realized what Jesus had done, the atmosphere of outrage in the hall became positively stifling.

At this point, the guide instructed me to let the scene fade from my inner vision, until only Jesus and I were left. "What do you say to Him?", she asked.

For a moment, I had no idea what to say—until a revelation came crashing in upon me like daylight into a dark cellar. *They aren't bad people are they?* I said to Jesus. *All these people hating You, hating the woman, so narrow in scope and rigid in their beliefs—they aren't bad people. These are the people I buy horseradish and shoo-fly pie from, people I've sung and prayed with. They're just people, insecure and scared and doing the best they can. They aren't evil.* And as I said it, I began to weep—great racking sobs for all the years I had sat in judgment on "those backward people." I had said "Aha—see?" when someone vandalized a Lancaster synagogue, but been silent when over eighty people arrived to clean up the damage. When local residents fought against the establishment of Lancaster County's first gay-friendly church, I shook my head in self-righteous disgust; when a Church of the Brethren pastor stepped forward to broker a peace accord between the church and the borough, I said nothing.

And even if these people hadn't had what I consider "redeeming characteristics," who am I that anyone should need to be redeemed in my eyes?

I am a mysterious to them as they are to me, aren't they? I said to my Lord. *They aren't bad people.*

Since then, I have refrained from dismissing any spiritual practice out-of-hand, thinking that it "wouldn't work for me." Every time a new idea makes its way through, it opens a little breach in depression's hardened wall of impossibility; every time an idea I had accepted as axiomatic dissolves, it opens up a little space in which to move and breathe.

-Chapter 32-

Magical Thinking in a Miraculous World[xxiii]

It is quite possible that an animal has spoken civilly to me and I didn't catch the remark because I wasn't paying attention. Children pay better attention than grownups. If Fern says that the animals in Zuckerman's barn talk, I'm quite ready to believe her. Perhaps if people talked less, animals would talk more. –E. B. White, *Charlotte's Web*

...a mouse is miracle enough to stagger sextillions of infidels. –Walt Whitman, "Song of Myself"

* * *

I have been making the case that mindfulness can be a highly effective way of dealing with depression, and it seems to me that one of the greatest barriers people face in practicing mindfulness—particularly people of a religious turn of mind—is that we are constantly on the lookout for something extraordinary, to the point that we miss ordinary beauty and blessing. Surrounded by the miraculous, we have eyes only for the magical.

Stage magicians Penn and Teller caused a stir in the magic world when they began showing audiences how tricks were done. This worked because, contrary to what you might expect, taking the magic out of the trick didn't actually...take the magic out. When the audience saw what was really happening, they were as amazed by the reality as by the illusion.

I believe that miracles work mostly in the same way:

God allows us to see the depth behind the everyday existence of which we usually see only the surface. And the reality is more astonishing than the illusion. Take, for example, the dramatic conclusion to the cycle of stories about Elijah.

And it came about when the LORD was about to take up Elijah by a whirlwind to heaven...Elijah said to Elisha, "Ask what I shall do for you before I am taken from you." And Elisha said, "Please, let a double portion of your spirit[23] be upon me." He said, "You have asked a hard thing. Nevertheless, if you see me when I am taken from you, it shall be so for you; but if not, it shall not be so." As they were going along and talking, behold, there appeared a chariot of fire and horses of fire which separated the two of them. And Elijah went up by a whirlwind to heaven. Elisha saw it and cried out, "My father, my father, the chariots of Israel and its horsemen!" And he saw Elijah no more. (2 Kings 2:1, 9b-12a, NASB)*

Elijah told Elisha that he would become his spiritual heir *if he saw him*—which implies to me that Elisha might well *not* have seen a chariot and horses of fire come to take Elijah up to heaven in a whirlwind. If Elijah would have been taken up that way whether Elisha saw it or not, the miracle is not in the occurrence, but in the *seeing*. Like Penn and Teller, God allowed Elisha to see the way it was actually done.

Another, more recent example: the nineteenth century Russian monk Seraphim of Sarov, after fifteen years of austerities in a hermitage, moved back to the monastery when, because of his reputation for holiness and wonder-

---

[23] A first-born son inherited twice as much of his father's property as his brothers; Elisha was asking Elijah to make him his spiritual heir.

working, people began to seek him out in his retreat. He took on the role of a *staretz*, or spiritual advisor.

One day, sensing that he was having trouble getting through to a disciple, he took the young man by the shoulders and said, "Look at me." The disciple told Seraphim he couldn't bear to look at him, because lightening was coming from his eyes and he appeared to be all aflame. Seraphim told the disciple that he was able to see him in that way because *God had opened his eyes*. Once again, it's evident that someone else might have been in the room also and seen nothing unusual—the *seeing* was the miracle.

So when we read some pious legend about a friar surprising St. Francis at his prayers and seeing him levitating or whatnot, the relevant question, it seems, is not "what actually happened?" but "what did the informant actually experience, and what does it mean that he or she experienced it?" The spiritual reality is always active behind the visible reality—we are surrounded by a "great cloud of witnesses." A miracle is when we're enabled to peek behind the curtain.

Of course, what we can actually see every day is pretty miraculous, too. In *Charlotte's Web*, Dr. Dorian gives Mrs. Arable his take on the "miraculous" writing in the spider's web:

I don't understand it. But for that matter I don't understand how a spider learned to spin a web in the first place. When the words appeared, everyone said they were a miracle. But nobody pointed out that the web itself is a miracle. (White 109)

The web is White's symbol for the miraculous within the everyday. But what exactly is a "symbol"? Well, the word "symbol" comes from two Greek words meaning "thrown together." When two friends were about to be parted, they would break an animal bone, each of them keeping one half as a symbol of the other. In other words, the symbol you hold in your hand is only half of a reality, the other half of which is elsewhere—and the two halves symbolically throw the two of you together.

I think the phenomenal world is sown with symbols of the spiritual—effulgences of the hidden world that burst forth into the visible one. Why else should there be music? Or flowers? Notwithstanding all the valid evolutionary explanations about bees and pollination, the fantastic blue of delphiniums is here for us because God just couldn't help himself. And the other half of that symbol is with God, and can throw us together with God if we let it.

So we needn't be on the watch for something overtly extraordinary. A spider's web or bird's nest, photosynthesis, azaleas and the wonders of the human brain—we can explain them to an extent, but we can never explain them *away*. They are miraculous, and on our very best days, we can see that. The Zen master Hakuin said, "Not knowing how near the truth is, we seek it far away. We are like one who, in the midst of water, cries out in thirst so piteously; we are like the children of a rich man who wandered away among the poor." We often miss the miracles because we are looking for magic. Maybe if we talk less, the universe will talk more.

Contemplative awareness is the "being here now" that allows us to hear the universe talk by really and fully experiencing our lives as we live them. We spend so much of our time remembering the past and anticipating the future, being anywhere and anywhen else than we actually are—and I find that this exacerbates depression like nothing else. When I am caught in a spiral of negative thinking, whether backward-looking sadness or forward-looking anxiety, the best thing I can possibly do is to get out of my head and into my body, my surroundings, and the present moment—no matter how unfulfilling the present moment may look.

"The world is charged with the grandeur of God," wrote Gerard Manley Hopkins; the problem is that the world *looks* so ordinary. I fear that one of the results of spirituality that overemphasizes technique is that it fosters a Transcendent Divinity mindset—the belief that God is outside ourselves and separate from us, and that we must attain to divine union by struggling to "find" God. All of which may have truth in it—but only part of the truth. The ordinary world is already miraculous; we needn't be on the lookout for the extraordinary.

Take, for example, the story of St. Francis of Assisi and the leper.

For indeed at one time the sight of lepers was (as he used to say) so bitter to him that when in the days of his vanity he looked at their houses about two miles off, he stopped his nostrils with his hands. But when now by the grace and power of the Highest he was beginning to think of holy and profitable things, one day, while still in the habit of the world, he met a leper, and, having become stronger than himself, went near and kissed him. (Celano)

Later versions of this simple story embroidered it with conventional pieties, among them being the Lord Jesus visiting Francis in a dream that night, informing him that the leper was actually Himself in disguise.

Similarly, there is St. Christopher, who, according to one thirteenth-century account, found a child by the river who begged him to take him across. Christopher lifted the boy onto his shoulders, and as he began the crossing, the river rose and swelled, and the child became as heavy as lead, until Christopher began to fear they would both be drowned.

And when he was escaped with great pain, and passed the water, and set the child aground, he said to the child: Child, thou hast put me in great peril; thou weighest almost as I had all the world upon me, I might bear no greater burden. And the child answered: Christopher, marvel thee nothing, for thou hast not only borne all the world upon thee, but thou hast borne him that created and made all the world, upon thy shoulders. I am Jesu Christ the king, to whom thou servest in this work. And because that thou know that I say to be the truth, set thy staff in the earth by thy house, and thou shalt see tomorrow morn that it shall bear flowers and fruit, and anon he vanished from his eyes. And then Christopher set his staff in the earth, and when he arose on the morn, he found his staff like a palmier bearing flowers, leaves and dates. (Voragine)

I could have seriously used some signs and wonders like those when, in the dead of one snowy winter, while my children were still toddlers, our family took a young immigrant woman, her two-year-old daughter, and her two-week-old son into our home. When we learned that this friend-of-friends was losing her apartment and had nowhere to go, my wife and I wished briefly that our modest property had an outlying carriage house like the grand homes on the more fashionable end of our Philadelphia neighborhood. But recalling that God didn't charge us to "take the homeless poor into your carriage house" (see Isaiah 58:6-7), we opened our hearts and our rooms to the adrift little family. I now understand why we need to make up stories about Jesus appearing to do-gooders after their good-doing and assure them that they had done good. Jesus Himself tells us "whatever you did for one of the least of these brothers and sisters of mine, you did for me" (Matthew 25:40), so we shouldn't need any reminders. But it would certainly be easier if we got them.

But on the other hand, I think stories like this have a liability, in that they persuade us to half-expect some miraculous visitation whenever God has an assignment for us—and this blinds us to the opportunities around us in our day-to-day lives, deafens us to God's call to us through "the least of these," and leaves us insensible to the divine grandeur with which the world is charged.

---

xxiii "Magical Thinking in a Miraculous World" first appeared in *Elephant Journal* on February 16, 2011, in a slightly different form. Used here by permission.

-Chapter 33-

The Home Version of Our Game^{xxiv}

This is the first thing I wrote after quitting my teaching job. It was one of my most popular blog posts, so it evidently resonated with a lot of people. From the vantage point of the householder—someone living "in the world," as opposed to an intentional religious community like an abbey, convent or ashram—householders face greater challenges in consciously cultivating their spiritual lives. The fact that most of the better-known books on spiritual practice are written by monks, nuns or clergy can make them seem out of touch with the day-to-day lives of ordinary people.

But while some monastics do indeed devote a large amount of their time to prayer, spiritual direction and contemplative practice, many spend a lot of time changing bedpans and soiled sheets, cooking, cleaning, and generally caring for others on a very demanding schedule. Franciscan friars, for instance, have always had "day jobs," in Francis's time it was usually as casual farm day-laborers, while today it may be anything from baker to university faculty.

My point being that, as well-received as the piece was when I wrote it, it does lack balance; living in community is hard work, and can scarcely be characterized as being "carried to the skies on flow'ry beds of ease," as the old hymn says. The fact that there may be a dearth of books on the spiritual life written by lay people doesn't imply that the professed religious don't "get it" about life "in the world." However, since this piece represents a turning point in my own thought about spiritual practice, I include it here in its original, if possibly biased, form.

Looking at reviews on Amazon of a book I was considering buying, I came across this gem:

I keep waiting for the day when someone writes a version of Buddhism for the working mom. I think that person should herself be a mother with at least one ADHD child. She should be clinically depressed and have a couch potato for a husband. If she manages to help the child grow into someone with a good marriage and a real profession, I'll buy all of her books. Unfortunately what we keep getting are philosophies created by self-satisfied, introverted, childless, hermits like (XXXXX). There is nothing wrong with an introverted, childless, hermit being self-satisfied. What is wrong is suggesting that his way of being represents THE path to enlightenment for everyone.

I see the reviewer's point: many writers on spiritual topics do seem to be either members of religious orders or unattached people who can order their days more as they wish than we in the married-with-children crowd can.

As I sit on my porch writing this, I can hear my five- and seven-year-old daughters playing inside the house. While they were in school, I was able to meditate twice a day. Now, while they are home for the summer, I read the Office of Morning Prayer and, if I'm lucky, doze off during meditation before bedtime.

And vexingly enough, when I have the flexibility to do what I need to in order to present my best self to the world, I only see my children a few hours a day; when I scarcely have time for practice at all, I have them with me hour after hour. They are, I think, not the better for it.

—Hang on…

OK, here's what I'm talking about: I just had to go change the bedclothes after one of my girls got so involved in an audiobook that she put off going to the bathroom until she wet herself—and because I am not *yet* the Worst

Dad in the World, I did *not* say, "You did WHAT? How freaking old are you, child?" But I thought it. I'm pretty sure that never happened to Thomas Merton.

But here's my point: while hermits and free spirits may have it easier than householders in some ways, I think there is an Absolute Value of Practice in everybody's life, and that practice can be neither created nor destroyed. The big difference is this: what we all do—householders, hermits and the unattached—on the black mat is mere scrimmage; the game is what happens everywhere else. The difference between "them" and "us" is that we don't get as much dedicated scrimmage time, and so must do more of our practice "in game."

—Wait, hang on…

OK—and I am not making this up—my wife is being admitted to the hospital because an injury she received last week (an upholstery nail clean through her thumb) has become infected, and the infection has become systemic, so they're going to put her on IV antibiotics and possibly operate, so I'll be taking the children to grandma's house by myself tonight, I guess.

I'm told that Tibetan Buddhist monks meditate in the charnel pits; I've read that Swamis meditate in the cremation grounds. My life isn't set up for me to do *either* of those things right now. I have to settle for taking Communion to elderly people in nursing homes—which *is* great practice, too—when I am paying attention—and has the added benefit of giving comfort and a sense of connectedness to a living person, while I contemplate mortality and the dissolution of form.

I drove my children to Hershey, where we had

planned a weekend with my wife's family, then drove back to Philadelphia to be near my wife, the patient. There was a certain amount of medical drama, the relation of which would compromise my quality of life at home, but though she would have been dead by now had this happened in our grandparents' time, she is just fine now. As I watched her sleeping on the hospital bed, her bandaged hand suspended from the IV pole, her drawn face pale above the tangle of thin blankets and her gown askew on shoulders that looked frail in the weird hospital half-light, I reached into my pocket for my rosary.

Then I changed my mind.

I sat down and, for a long time, simply looked mindfully at my wife and the mother of my children, breathed in and out and let go of all thoughts. I cannot describe the experience in words, but I can say that I was present, that the frailty and freakish blessedness of human life was contemplated, and that practice happened.

Of course, every life has drama and exigency; it isn't the press of events that makes a householders' life challenging, but the press of non-events, the minutiae of day-to-day life.

A recent update from one of my Facebook friends:

_____*is totally overwhelmed by all the little details of her life: buy stuff for XXXX's camps, reschedule orthodontist, find few last props for (the play), clean house and look for new car. I need a personal manager.*

This is what Sri Ramakrishna, the nineteenth century Bengali saint whom many consider an Incarnation of God, meant when he praised the householder who also managed to be a *bhakta,* or devotee:

A devotee who can call upon God while living a householder's life is a hero indeed. God thinks, 'He who has renounced the world for My sake will surely pray to Me...But he is blessed indeed who prays to Me in the midst of his worldly duties...Such a man is a real hero." (M)

The real challenge for us sheet-changers/dog-poop-scoopers/grocery-shoppers/pediatrician-appointment-makers is to find the practice in the game that sometimes leaves us little time or energy for scrimmage.

Swami Vivekananda told of a young hermit who, after several years of ascetic spiritual exercises in the forest, one day felt a shower of twigs fall on his head as he meditated under a tree. Looking up, he saw a crane and a crow fighting in the tree, and as he inwardly cursed them for disturbing him, fire shot forth from his head and consumed the birds. Elated at his new power, he went as usual into the village to beg his food. At the first house he approached, a woman's voice within bade him wait. "How dare she make me wait?" the hermit thought. "She does not yet know my power."

Again he heard the woman's voice from within: "Boy, do not be thinking too highly of yourself; here is neither crane nor crow!"

When the woman finally received him, the chastened hermit asked how she had known his thoughts.

"My boy, I do not know your Yoga or your practices. I am a common everyday woman. I made you wait because my husband is ill, and I was nursing him. All my life I have struggled to do my duty. When I was unmarried, I did my duty to my parents; now that I am married, I do my duty to my husband; that is all the Yoga I practice. But by doing my duty I have become illumined; thus I could read your thoughts

and know what you had done in the forest. (Vivekananda, Karma Yoga 52)

I cannot yet say that I match this woman's zeal—but it's surely a worthy goal. I'm going to bed. I will not be meditating tonight.

---

xxiv "The Home Version of Our Game" first appeared under the title "I Will Not Be Meditating Tonight: Family Life as Spiritual Practice" in *Elephant Journal* on July 13, 2010, in a slightly different form. Used here by permission.

-Chapter 34-

Going Off My Meds[xxv]

Meditation is one of the few things that can be done well in the midst of depression, because all if requires of is that we sit down, be quiet, and pay attention. –Philip Martin, *The Zen Path Through Depression*

The various practices of kriya yoga…help you to attain a state of peace and tranquility without beating, kicking and abusing the mind. –Swami Sivananda Saraswati, *Kundalini Yoga Tantra*

* * *

Before I got my depression treated, my meditation practice was going great. I could sit in Centering Prayer (a modern revival of an ancient Christian contemplative practice) in external and internal stillness for a half-hour or more—in fact, I loved doing it and looked forward to it. But when I started taking anti-depressants, I found myself simply unable to quiet the mind without giving it something to do. Things are better now, but still not as good as they were before I sought treatment—and maybe they never will be.

A recent article in *Tricycle* showed me I was not alone in this:

After a few weeks on an SSRI she surfaced from her depression; but now she was buzzing, and her zazen was affected. "I got this tremendous surge, like caffeine, which stirred up thoughts and ideas. I had agitated, random, distracting thoughts and a ringing in my ears. It was really hard to meditate, hard to settle the waters. At first I couldn't count my breath for even ten seconds. It was almost like being a beginner again." After her brain adapted to the antidepressant, the buzziness subsided, and her mind settled down. (Hooper)

The initial "buzziness" subsided for me, too, but not enough to bring back the ability I had as a depressed person to slip into contemplative consciousness for substantial periods.

This is not a universal sequence of events; in fact, the opposite is often the case.

One comment I heard again and again is that depression makes it difficult if not impossible to practice—which is not surprising given that "inability to concentrate" appears prominently on the Hamilton Depression Rating Scale used by psychiatrists in diagnosis... When depressed people try to meditate...a major part of their meditative energy is going into fighting depression. Instead of letting it take them forward, they are using their meditation as an attempt to self-medicate. The bulk of their energy may go into obsessive ruminations or attempts to process emotional pain that feels stuck. They are facing a gradient that is too steep. (Hooper)

This was not my experience—perhaps because, for a long time, I didn't realize that I was depressed. I just thought everything sucked. And the time between my identifying the problem and seeking treatment for it was very brief, so perhaps I didn't have time to develop the habit of using meditation as self-medication.

For a long time, I resisted actual medication because I thought it was "cheating." More than once I went off my meds as soon as I felt better, and it was always a mistake. But the belief that I ought to be able to do without was deeply ingrained. If I were really all spiritual and stuff, I ought to be able to meditate my way out of this, right? This type of thinking can be a big obstacle for people on a spiritual path, as one's emotional state is often taken as evidence of spiritual attainment. During a retreat with a group of college students who grew up in missionary families, several of them reported experiencing intense pressure while growing up to "always be cheerful in front of your non-Christian friends."

I wonder what these kids' missionary parents would have thought of the wild mood swings of Francis of Assisi? Or St. John of the Cross's prolonged "dark night of the soul"? Or Henri Nouwen's depression, or Mother Teresa's?

My wife, a physician, thinks Francis was bi-polar—and he did have periods of intense exaltation alternating with times of deep depression. But I'm not sure that diagnosis covers it, because he also did a lot of things that seem just plain loopy. I often imagine, for instance, what it must have been like to be traveling with him on the day he left the road to *preach to the birds.*

"Father Francis, where are you...can we...what is he...he isn't...*Oh. My. God.*"

From here, of course, it's only a short step to the realization that most people who are generally recognized as holy have been perceived as crazy; even Jesus' family "went to take charge of him, for they said, 'He is out of his mind.'" (Mark3:21) And I've often wondered what would have happened to Hildegard of Bingen's visions if she could have gotten her migraines managed, or if Joan of Arc had been treated for the psychosis that anyone who heard voices in the church bells would surely be diagnosed with today. Would our spiritual heritage be the poorer for it? Are we "curing" people of sainthood with Zoloft?

...[I]f long-term meditators are known to experience dark nights of the soul or desert wastelands on the path, how is one to know if one's suffering is from one of the warning signs of a debilitating illness or simply piercing the veils of illusion? Is the characteristic "hollowness" and "emptiness" of clinical depression altogether different from the experience of shunyata? *By mistaking a glimpse of* shunyata *for a symptom of depression, might one risk medicating away the early stages of nirvana?*

Just as it is naive to imagine meditation as a panacea for all psychological ills, perhaps it is a Western prejudice to insist that an enlightened master should be the picture of what we consider perfect mental health. Gelek Rinpoche tells a story about a very high lama in Tibet who suffered from a serious mental illness—probably bipolar illness or schizophrenia—and periodically behaved bizarrely. His mental illness did not seem to impair his spiritual status. (Hooper)

Now, while I am the last person to compare myself with any of these great spiritual luminaries, it does seem clear to me that my depression, while it was making my family miserable and therefore needed to be treated, wasn't as much of an impediment to my spiritual practice as the treatment has been.

So now I am apt to meditate in ways that involve doing stuff: mentally repeating a passage of Scripture, repeating a *mantra,* chanting the Psalms, praying the rosary, praying the Compline (Night Prayer) service from the *Book of Common Prayer,* singing my own devotional songs— anything to give the busy puppy of my mind something to chew on.

One thing I had never found useful was *pranayama,* the yogic methods of harnessing the *prana,* or life force, through control of the breath. In theory, it's supposed to work something like this story from India:

A man was being held prisoner in a tall tower with only one window. When his wife stood under the window and called out to him, asking what she could do for him, he told her to bring some thread, some twine, some rope, some honey and a horned beetle.

When his wife returned with the items, the man instructed her to tie the thread to the beetle and put a drop of honey on each of its horns. The beetle began climbing the tower to get at the honey, until the man was able to reach out the window and catch it. He then told his wife to tie the twine to the thread, and when he had hauled the thread into his cell, her instructed her to tie the rope to the twine. He then pulled up the twine and the rope and used the latter to lower himself out the window to freedom.

We are the prisoners of our thoughts and feelings, and *pranayama* is meant to free us in a way analogous the this prisoner's method; if we can "get hold" of the breath—the thread—we can then control the body—the twine. Having got hold of the body, we can control the mind—the rope. Then we can free ourselves.

The problem is, most pranayama involves holding the breath, which I hate. It goes against all my years of training as a singer and performer, and besides, it makes me twitch. I am more simpatico with the advice an old voice teacher once gave me: "I believe in breathing a lot all the time." But I have found a method of pranayama that not only encourages plenty of breathing, but is a marvelous antidote for the anxiety that dogs the steps of depression.

Yogi Bhajan, who introduced Kundalini Yoga into the U.S., taught a *pranayama*-based *kriya* (action) called "When You Don't Know What to Do" that is so simple, you wouldn't think it would have any effect at all—but it does. After just a few seconds of this, my breathing deepens and slows way down, and my mind becomes calm and stable. I have taught this in workshops, and people almost always respond well to it.

There are several variants of this technique in circulation; I use the version in psychotherapist David-Shannahoff-Khalsa's *Sacred Therapies: The Kundalini Yoga Meditation Handbook for Mental Health* (Norton, 2012). I paraphrase it here:

Sit with a straight back, either cross-legged or in a chair. (Any comfortable cross-legged posture is fine.) Cross the hands with the right hand on top of the left, and the right thumb on top of the left thumb. Both palms face toward the chest, a few inches away from the sternum. With the eyes closed, focus on the space between the eyebrows (the *kshetra* of the *ajna chakra*, or "third eye) or at a point on the horizon. Then:

I.   Inhale through the nose; exhale through the nose.

II. Inhale through the mouth, with the lips pursed as if to whistle; relax the mouth and exhale.

III. Inhale through the nose; exhale through the relaxed mouth.

IV. Inhale through the mouth with lips pursed; exhale through the nose.

Repeat this sequence for 11 minutes and, if you wish, gradually work up to 31 minutes.

And that's it. This sublimely simple *kriya* showed me the fallacy of thinking that because I couldn't sit still with a quiet mind, I couldn't meditate. Try it yourself and see if it doesn't quiet your mind and calm your nerves.

But don't allow this, or any other technique that works—that makes you feel better—to lead you to believe that you needn't seek treatment. Practice and treatment are the two wings that get the bird of recovery off the ground. As John Tarrant, *roshi* of the California Diamond Sangha, puts it,

Teachings and practice can help you...but using dharma to affect a chemical balance is the long way round; it can be too late for some people. When there is a chemical imbalance in the body, it is a good idea to work with that chemically. (Hooper)

---

xxv "Going Off My Meds" was published on *Elephant Journal* on June 3, 2013, in a slightly different form. Used here by permission.

-Chapter 35-

Intercessory Prayer: "Holding in the Light"

We don't know what God wants us to pray for. But the Holy Spirit prays for us with groanings that cannot be expressed in words.
–Romans 8:26

* * *

It is said that prayer doesn't change God—it changes the one who prays. There have been a number of studies that seem to indicate better medical outcomes for patients who are prayed for, but one study from the National Center for Biotechnology Information seems to bear out the truth of this saying about those who pray. For "An experimental study of the effects of distant, intercessory prayer on self-esteem, anxiety, and depression," a randomized controlled clinical trial, ninety "agents," (prayers) were assigned 406 "subjects" (patients for whom to pray.) Eleven outcomes were measured, and after twelve weeks, all the subjects were found to have significantly improved in all eleven areas. But here's the really relevant part for our purposes: *the agents also significantly improved in ten of the areas.* In fact, "(a)gents had significantly better scores than did subjects on all objective measures." (O'Laoire) Intercessory prayer—praying for other people—really is good for you, apparently.

And some people are good at intercessory prayer. They remember, not only those who have asked them for prayer, but also those whose situations simply seem to warrant it. They pray fluently, simply and without over-thinking things, and they make their needs known without seeming to micromanage God.

I am not one of those people.

In a group setting—in church, during the Daily Office with my fellow Franciscans, after Morning Meditation—it's easy to simply ask for prayer for someone and briefly describe their situation and needs. But when alone, I feel the need to "pray something," and find myself either talking too much, or feeling like I'm just going through the motions. I wonder whether to pray for a particular outcome, or simply "Your will be done." Then I get caught in a "your Father knows what you need before you ask" loop (Matthew 6:8), wondering if there's even any point to intercession.

For those who may have similar difficulties, I will share a technique I have developed to deepen my intercessory prayer life using the Rosary.

Before beginning, I spend about five minutes in silent meditation, being aware of my intention to use the practice as a vehicle for intercession. Then, during each Hail Mary I allow the remembrance of some person or situation to come into my awareness. I then simply "hold them in the Light," as the Quakers say, for the duration of the prayer, trusting that God will take it from there.

And that's it.

The "allowing" is key; if I sit down with a pre-determined list of people to pray for, the whole practice takes on a mechanical, even frantic aspect—and once I've prayed through the list, my mind goes blank. (One exception to this principle is when I've had a spate of requests for prayer; when that happens, I do make a list—though I often find that the simple act of writing the requests down helps me to remember them without recourse to the list during the prayer time.)

Over-thinking is deadly. It's important to be like Pooh, and wait for things to come to us, rather than Rabbit, who takes it upon himself to go out and get them. This requires trust, but the trust is always rewarded; I have never done this practice without a steady stream of friends, enemies, relations, colleagues and situations coming to mind to be held up in prayer.

I do this practice with the Dominican Rosary, because each group of beads (or "decade," so called because they are arranged in groups of ten) is associated with a particular "mystery" from the lives of Jesus and Mary. The mysteries[24] are:

THE JOYFUL MYSTERIES

Traditionally prayed on Monday, Thursday, and Sunday in Advent and Christmas.

The Annunciation of Mary

The Archangel Gabriel appears to Mary, telling her of God's plan for her to give birth to Jesus. (Luke 1: 26-38)

The Visitation of Mary to her cousin Elizabeth

Mary visits her older cousin, who is also pregnant with John the Baptizer. This passage is the source of the liturgical canticle known as the *Magnificat*. (Luke 1: 39-56)

The Birth of Jesus

God enters the world in the form of an infant. (Luke 2: 6-20; Matthew 1:18-25)

---

[24] Pope John Paul II added a group of ten "Luminous Mysteries" that reference Jesus' public ministry, but they are not in universal use.

The Presentation of Jesus in the Temple

Because under Jewish law all first-born "belong to the Lord," Mary and Joseph take Jesus to the Temple forty days after his birth to "redeem" him with the sacrifice of two doves. This passage is the source of the liturgical canticle known as the *Nunc Dimittis*. (Luke 2: 22-39)

THE SORROWFUL MYSTERIES

Traditionally prayed on Tuesday, Friday and Sundays during Lent.

The Agony in the Garden of Gethsemane
Jesus prays on the Mount of Olives on the night before His crucifixion. (Matthew 26: 36-46; Mark 14:32-42; Luke 22: 39-46)
The Scourging at the Pillar
A form of torture routinely applied before crucifixion. (Matthew 27:26; Mark 15:15; John 19:1)
The Crowning with Thorns
The soldiers mock the "King of the Jews." (Matthew 27:29-30; Mark 15:16-20; John 1: 2-3)
The Carrying of the Cross
The condemned carried the crosspiece to the site of execution. (Luke 23: 26-32; Matthew 27:31-32; Mark 15:21)
The Crucifixion
(Matthew 27: 33-54; Mark 15: 22-39; Luke 23: 33-47; John 19: 17-37)

THE GLORIOUS MYSTERIES

Traditionally prayed on Wednesday, Saturday and Sundays during Easter and Pentecost.

The Resurrection of Jesus
> (Matthew 28: 1-10; Mark 16: 1-18; Luke 24: 1-49;
> John 20:1-29)

The Ascension of Jesus
> (Mark: 16: 19-20; Luke 24: 50-51; Acts 1: 6-11)

The Sending of the Holy Spirit at Pentecost
> (Acts 2: 1-41)

The Assumption of Mary[25]

The Crowning of Mary as Queen of Heaven
> (See Revelation 12:1-2 on the last two mysteries.)

In the traditional practice, one thinks about these events while praying the ten Hail Mary's in each decade. But I have never gotten used to such discursive meditation; I don't like "thinking about" things during contemplative prayer time. So while I soldiered on with the Rosary off and on for years, brief seasons of great fruitfulness alternated with endless stretches of mechanical recitation, and I would often abandon the practice for long periods.

When I use the Rosary as an aid to intercession, however, the practice comes powerfully to life, because the mysteries themselves guide my intercessions. While praying the Annunciation, for instance, ten people or groups of people who are struggling with issues of vocation may come to mind; during the Birth of Jesus decade, I remember expectant mothers and new parents; as I pray the Carrying of the Cross, I remember people who have taken on extraordinary burdens. And while you wouldn't think you

---

[25] Because, as a non-Catholic, I do not believe in the Assumption—or taking up bodily into heaven—of Mary while still alive, I substitute the Orthodox "Dormition", or "falling asleep" (death) of Mary for this mystery.

know 150 people, groups or situations in need of your prayer, you would probably be surprised. Just relax and refrain from grasping (as the Buddhists say) and they will come to you. And don't worry—you will not forget those people who have particularly solicited your intercession.

So this practice has not only grounded and freed my intercessory prayer, but it has also enlivened my use of the Rosary. For me, holding people in the light whose situations connect them to the mysteries is a much more meaningful meditation on those mysteries than forcing myself to think about the events in some more literal way, while remembering those for whom I pray in the light of Jesus' and Mary's lives and ministries enables me to pray for others without getting tangled up in what to say.

Finally, after this practice, I have a vivid sense of the "great cloud of witnesses" (Hebrews 12:1) by whom we are all surrounded on our spiritual pilgrimage; I feel more connected to "all the faithful of every generation"[26] in the Communion of Saints, and am powerfully reassured that I am not alone. For a person living with depression—in which both the feeling and the fact of social isolation are often major components—this can be powerful medicine.

---

[26] *Book of Common Prayer*

-Chapter 36-

The Fires of the Senses

God is the offering, the One Who offers, and the fire that consumes.
–Bhagavad Gita 4:24

* * *

This is a wholly idiosyncratic mindfulness practice; you will not find this in any of the classic literature on mindfulness. But I find it a great mood-lifter.

I was walking through Center City Philadelphia on my way to a panel discussion on Creating Sacred Music. As I was feeling neither especially sacred nor particularly musical, I cast about for a way to get into the right frame of mind.

Looking at all the colorful sights of the city, I remembered how, when my children were babies, everything I saw, heard, smelled or tasted would remind me of them. "Clare would like those flowers," I'd think; street buskers would make me wish Sophie were with me; foods brought one or the other kid to mind, depending on their taste.

What if I could broadcast my experience directly into their minds, I thought, so they could experience my walk vicariously? Then I realized that we are called upon, in the Bhagavad Gita, to do more or less exactly that—with God as the audience of our sensory input:

Some yogis perfectly worship the demigods by offering different sacrifices to them, and some of them offer sacrifices in the fire of the Supreme

Brahman.

Some [the unadulterated brahmacaris] sacrifice the hearing process and the senses in the fire of mental control, and others [the regulated householders] **sacrifice the objects of the senses in the fire of the senses.**

Others, who are interested in achieving self-realization through control of the mind and senses, offer the functions of all the senses, and of the life breath, as oblations into the fire of the controlled mind. (Bhagavad Gita 4:24-27; emphasis added)

As I walked along, I mentally transmitted all the sights and sounds to Jesus, as though He were looking out through my eyes and hearing through my ears. As I walked along, exercising this "control of the mind and senses" by offering "the objects of the senses" into the fires of perception, I not only felt extremely close to the Lord, but I found my usual way of seeing people—a highly judgmental and evaluative way in which I am subject and everyone else is object—giving way to a compassionate mode of seeing as Christ sees.

"Christ has no body now on earth but yours," wrote St. Teresa of Avila:

No hands, no feet on earth but yours. Yours are the eyes through which he looks compassion on this world. Yours are the feet with which he walks about doing good. Yours are the hands, with which he blesses all the world.

Tantra takes the relation of the senses to their

objects even a step further, making the act of perceiving reflect the divine union of Shiva (the divine masculine and pure consciousness) and Shakti (the divine feminine and pure energy.)

A faculty and its object are like the primordial couple. The relationship of the eye to what is seen is the relationship of Shiva to his shakti. The ear and music, the eye and art, the tongue and flavour, all senses and their sensations are a participation in the eternal embrace. (Dupuche 58)

The body and the senses can be made the locus of divine service by an act of will by which we use them on God's behalf. This act sanctifies both the senses and their objects, bringing us a greater awareness of the divine presence within and without, and preparing us to "be an instrument of [God's] peace." Going a step further, St. Teresa found such a dedicating of the senses to be a way toward divine union, in which Christ——the "bridegroom" of her Carmelite soul——entered into her and lived His risen life through her:

I was reflecting upon how arduous a life this is…I said to myself, "Lord, give me some means by which I may put up with this life." He replied, "Think, daughter, of how after it is finished you will not be able to serve me in ways you can now. Eat for Me and sleep for Me, and let everything you do be for Me, as though you no longer lived but I; for this is what St. Paul was speaking of." (Avila 361)

On Martin Luther King Day of 2015, thirty-five members of my parish joined thousands of other activists in the #ReclaimMLK march in Philadelphia. We marched for an increase in the minimum wage, full, fair funding for public schools, and an end to racism and police brutality. We gathered at the school district office building before marching to the Constitution Center, and as I arrived early, I had plenty of time during which to practice this mindfulness technique, which I have come to call "inviting Jesus into my eyes." This time, however, I looked at people rather than just my general surroundings. As I offered up to Jesus the sight of all sorts and conditions of my fellow human beings, I was rewarded with wave upon wave of the sense of God's love for them. As Jesus looked out through my eyes, I was enabled to see through God's, and the divine love rolling back to me through the people I saw was almost like a physical thing.

Something of what I was experiencing must have shown in my face in some way, for whenever I made eye contact with one of my fellow marchers, instead of looking away awkwardly, I found them smiling at me—almost as though they could sense the divine love coming from me as I could sense it coming from them. I have done this many times since, and I always experience that love as I offer the sight of God's people up to God. It makes me feel less alone, more connected, more beloved, more of a divine instrument. God loves in me, feels in me, and I in God.

Thomas Traherne, the 17th-century Anglican mystic, must have experienced this mutual feeling-exchange in a very similar way, for he captured it in a way I recognized immediately from my own experience:

He is happy in you, when you are happy: as parents in their children. He is afflicted in all your afflictions. And whosoever toucheth you, toucheth the apple of His eye. Will you not be happy in all His enjoyments? He feeleth in you; will you not feel in Him? (Traherne 12)

Chapter 37

The Pearl of Great Price[xxvi]

For the beauty of the earth,
for the glory of the skies,
for the love which from our birth
over and around us lies;
Lord of all, to thee we raise
this our hymn of grateful praise.
–Folliot S. Pierpoint

* * *

I love Thanksgiving because it celebrates gratitude, and that is one of the most potent spiritual virtues one can cultivate, as well as a powerful anodyne for melancholy. If I were to add up all the minutes I have spent in ministry and break them down by activity, I think I spend the most time listening to dying people tell me how blessed they were—how grateful for their wonderful lives, their wonderful spouses and children, their jobs, and the exemplary care they were getting in their last days. I am privileged to be around people ending their lives in peace and gratitude. It is truly humbling, given the relative severity of their problems and mine; there was a strange beauty in it, something that called to the soul, whispering of harmony and rightness. There is pain in it, too—not in the dying, but in the gratitude: the pain one feels in the presence of beauty.

Every fall when I was growing up, my family would find a reason to drive out among the fantastic colors of the Upstate New York autumn. My mom in particular would be transported over the reds, oranges and golds on the wooded hillsides between our home in Syracuse and her native Pennsylvania. Every few minutes she would exclaim, "Oh, it's just so beautiful I can hardly stand it!"

On the face of it, this response to beauty seems strange, yet we have probably all felt that sort of pleasure that, in its intensity, verges on pain and which, notwithstanding, we can't get enough of. Anne Shirley, in Lucy Maud Montgomery's novel, felt the same sensation on her first sight of the spring flowers at Green Gables:

> *"It just satisfies me here"—she put one hand on her breast—"it made a queer funny ache and yet it was a pleasant ache...I have it lots of times—whenever I see anything royally beautiful."* (Montgomery 10)

Somerset Maugham identified the same ambiguous ache in his novel, *Of Human Bondage:*

> *Along one side lay the Cathedral with its great central tower, and Philip, who knew as yet nothing of beauty, felt when he looked at it a troubling delight which he could not understand...It gave him an odd feeling in his heart, and he did not know if it was pain or pleasure. It was the first dawn of the aesthetic emotion.* (Maugham 39)

Why should we ache in the presence of beauty? Why should the loveliness of either art or nature make us long for we know not what?

I am convinced that this movement of the soul has an exact counterpart in the body. What happens to us physically when we smell delicious food? We get hungry. What happens to us spiritually as we experience beauty? *We get hungry*. As the smell of cooking is the token of a feast for the body, whetting our appetite for the food that is the source of the aroma, so beauty is the token of a feast for the soul, whetting our appetite for the Source of beauty.

This, above all else, is why I seek God: just as the hunger of the body is meant to lead us to the body's sustenance, so the soul's hunger draws us toward the sustenance of the soul. If there were no such thing as food, there would be no such thing as hunger of the body—so because my soul hungers, I know that there is Bread of Heaven to satisfy it. Beauty is the aroma of the heavenly banquet.

Screwtape knew this, and did his best to warn his feckless nephew Wormwood of the power of beauty to undermine his demonic stratagems:

> *Even if we contrive to keep them ignorant of explicit religion, the incalculable winds of fantasy and music and poetry, the mere face of a girl, the song of a bird, or the sight of a horizon are always blowing our whole structure away...So inveterate is their appetite for Heaven...* (Lewis 156)

These "incalculable winds" bear the scent of the "feast of rich foods" promised by Isaiah. (Isaiah 25:6) God, I am convinced, draws us heavenward with this scent, just as the aroma of a pie in the old cartoons assumes the visible form of a beckoning arm that draws by the nose anyone within wafting range. We hunger, Paul Tillich tells us, in "anticipation of a fulfillment that cannot be found in an actual encounter." (Eusden) Simply put, because the smell is so good, we know the food must be even better—and because beauty moves us as it does, we know that beyond it must be something even more satisfying.

One reason I believe this is that Jesus, unlike other rabbis, sought out his disciples. Rather than setting up shop and attracting students as he acquired a reputation for holiness, which was the usual procedure, Jesus went out to the docks and dives and buttonholed his followers. "You did not choose me," he told them later, "but I chose you."

He talked about choosing in his parables, also:

> *The kingdom of heaven is like a treasure hidden in the field, which a man found and hid again; and from joy over it he goes and sells all that he has and buys that field. Again, the kingdom of heaven is like a merchant seeking fine pearls, and upon finding one pearl of great value, he went and sold all that he had and bought it.* (Matthew 13:45-6, NASB)

I think the second in this pair of parables—the kingdom of heaven as pearl merchant—is often misunderstood. We hear references to "the pearl of great price," but they often sound like the person making them thinks the term applies to the *kingdom*. Because the first parable likens the kingdom to a treasure worth acquiring at any cost, people seem to miss the point that in the second, *the kingdom is the merchant, not the pearl. We are the pearl.* It is *us* that God walks the dark hills to seek, and gives everything to acquire. And the beauty of the earth, the glory of the skies, the love of family and friends, spring flowers and autumn colors, music and poetry and birdsong are like the moon that reflects back to us the sunlight of God's love. Like the smell of Thanksgiving dinner, they are calling us home.

---

xxvi "Thanksgiving: The Pearl of Great Price" first appeared on *Elephant Journal* on October 19, 2011 in a slightly different form. Used here by permission.

Bibliography

Avila, Saint Teresa of. *The Collected Works of St. Teresa of Avila.* Ed. Kieran and Rodriguez, Otilio Kavanaugh. Trans. Kieran and Rodriguez, Otilio Kavanaugh. Vol. 1. ICS, 1976.

Balko, Radley. *Rise of the Warrior Cop: The Militarization of America's Police Forces.* PublicAffairs, 2014.

Boccio, Ian. *Mantra Yoga.*

Bosch, Torie. *Enough with the "Trophy Kid" Talk.* 6 July 2009. <http://www.slate.com/blogs/xx_factor/2009/07/06/the_trophies_that_supposedly_made_generation_y_so_entitled_didnt_inflate_our_egos.html>

Bridge, Jeffrey A. "Clinical Response and Risk for Reported Suicidal Ideation and Suicide Attempts in Pediatric Antidepressant Treatment: A Meta analysis of Randomized Controlled Trials." *JAMA* 297.15 (2007): 1683-1696.

Caldecott, Stratford. "Face to Face: The Difference Between Hindu and Christian Non-Dualism." *Communio: International Catholic Review* 34 (2007): 618.

Campbell, Joseph. *The Hero with a Thousand Faces.* New World Library, 2008.

Celano, Thomas of. *The First Life of St. Francis, by Thomas of Celano.* <http://www.indiana.edu/~dmdhist/francis.htm>

Chodron, Pema. *Pema Chodron.* <http://www.shambhala.org/teachers/pema/maitri1.php>

Dewan, Shaila. "For Professor, Fury Just Beneath the Surface." *The New York Times* 20 February 2010.

Dupuche, John. *Towards a Christian Tantra: The Interplay of Christianity and Kashmir Shaivism.* David Lovell Publishing, 2009.

Easwaran, Eknath. *The Mantram Handbook: A Practical Guide to Choosing Your Mantram and Calming Your Mind.* Nilgiri Press, 2008.

Eliot, George. *Adam Bede.* Penguin, 2008.

Eusden, John Dykstra and Westerhoff, John. *Sensing Beauty: Aesthetics, the Human Spirit, and the Church.* Pilgrim Press, 1998.

Foster, Jeff. *DIVINE SUICIDE: Depressive Breakdown as a Call to Awakening.* 2015. <http://www.lifewithoutacentre.com/writings/divine-suicide-depressive-breakdown-as-a-call-to-awakening/>

Goldstein, Elisha. *Uncovering Happiness: Overcoming Depression with Mindfulness and Self-Compassion.* Atria, 2015.

Hersh, Joshua. *In Israel, Spate Of Ultra-Orthodox Incidents Rattle The Secular Mainstream.* 12 January 2012. <http://www.huffingtonpost.com/2012/01/09/israel-orthodox-haredim_n_1190500.html>

Hooper, Judith. "Prozac & Enlightenment Mind Can antidepressants help or hinder waking up?" *Tricycle* Summer 1999.

Hudgins, Andrew. "Crucifixion—Montgomery, Alabama." *Upholding Mystery: An Anthology of Contemporary Christian Poetry.* Ed. David Impastato. Oxford University Press, 1996. 8.

Kabir. ""How Much is Not True"." *The Rag and Bone Shop of the Heart: A Poetry Anthology.* Ed. Robert Bly. Harper Perennial, 1993. 282.

Keillor, Garrison. "Al Denny." Keillor, Garrison. *The Book of Guys.* Penguin, 1994.

Keillor, Garrison. "The Babe." Keillor, Garrison. *Stories: An Audio Collection,* 1993.

Koval, Peter, et al. "Getting stuck in depression: The roles of rumination and emotional inertia ." *Cognition and Emotion* 26.8 (2012): 1412-1427.

Kuppens, Peter and Nicholas B., and Sheeber, Lisa Allen. "Emotional inertia and psychological maladjustment." *Psychological Science* 7 (2010): 984-991.

Kuppens, Peter, Allen, Nicholas B. and Sheeber, Lisa. "Emotional inertia and psychological maladjustment." *Psychological Science* 21.7 (2010): 984-991.

Laird, Martin. *Into the Silent Land: A Guide to the Christian Practice of Contemplation.* Oxford University Press, n.d.

Lewis, C.S. "Reflections on the Psalms." (1964): 136.

—. *The Screwtape Letters: How a Senior Devil Instructs a Junior Devil in the Art of Temptation.* Time, Inc., 1961.

M. *The Gospel of Sri Ramakrishna.* Trans. Swami Nikhilananda. Abridged. Ramakrishna-Vivekananda Center, 1988.

MacIntosh, Jean. "Steve gal: Self-love, not sex, is his woe." *New York Post* 20 February 2010.

Mahan, Brian. *Forgetting Ourselves on Purpose: Vocation and the Ethics of Ambition.* Jossey-Bass, 2002.

May, Gerald. *The Awakened Heart: Opening Yourself to the Love You Need.* HarperOne, 1993.

Meadows, Donella. *Thinking in Systems: A Primer.* Ed. Diana Wright. 2008.

Merton, Thomas. *No Man is an Island.* Mariner, n.d.

Miller, Arthur. "Tragedy and the Common Man." *The New York Times* 27 February 1949.

Monbiot, George. "The Age of Loneliness if Killing Us." *The Guardian* 14 October 2014.

Moore, Thomas. *Care of the Soul.* Harper Perennial, 1994.

NIMH. *"Care Managers" Help Depressed Elderly Reduce Suicidal Thoughts.* 2 March 2004. <http://www.nimh.nih.gov/news/science-news/2004/care-managers-help-depressed-elderly-reduce-suicidal-thoughts.shtml>

———. *New Therapies Show Promise for Vascular Depression; Heart, Metabolic, Risks of Some Antipsychotic Medications Flagged.* 7 May 2008.
<http://www.nimh.nih.gov/news/science-news/2008/new-therapies-show-promise-for-vascular-depression-heart-metabolic-risks-of-some-antipsychotic-medications-flagged.shtml>

———. *Primary Care Doctors May Overlook Elderly Patients' Mental Health.* 25 February 2008.
<http://www.nimh.nih.gov/news/science-news/2008/primary-care-doctors-may-overlook-elderly-patients-mental-health.shtml>

O'Laoire, S. "An experimental study of the effects of distant, intercessory prayer on self-esteem, anxiety, and depression." *Alternative Therapies in Health and Medicine* 6 (1997): 38-53.

Percy, Walker. *The Message in the Bottle: How Queer Man Is, How Queer Language Is, and What One Has to Do with the Other.* Open Road Media, 2011.

Postman, Neil. *The Disappearance of Childhood.* Vintage/Random House, 1994.

Pratchett, Terry. "The Wee Free Men." (2006): 155.

———. *Wintersmith.* Harper Collins, 2007.

Reiss, Mike. "What happens when everyone's a winner? Some ask whether feel-good trophies are actually good for children." *Boston Globe* 23 February 2006.

Rillito River Project. *The Water Table*. 2011.
<http://www.rillitoriverproject.org/introductionhistory-mission-and-vision/>

Rubinstein, Richard. *Aristotle's Children: How Christians, Muslims and Jews Rediscovered the Ancient Wisdom and Illuminated the Middle Ages*. Mariner, 2004.

Shane, Scott. "F.B.I., Laying Out Evidence, Closes Anthrax Case." *New York Times* 19 February 2010.

Solomon, Andrew. "Anatomy of Melancholy." *The New Yorker* 12 January 1998.

—. *The Noonday Demon: An Atlas of Depression*. Scribner, 2001.

Spurgeon, Charles. *The Treasury of David*.
<http://www.spurgeon.org/treasury/ps137.htm>

Steinbeck, John. *The Grapes of Wrath*. Penguin Classics, 2006.

Strauss, Claudia. *Talking to Depression: Simple Ways to Connect When Someone In Your Life Is Depressed*. NAL, 2004.

Styron, William. *Darkness Visible: A Memoir of Madness*. Vintage, 1992.

Suzuki, Shunryu. *Zen Mind, Beginner's Mind*. Shambala, 2006.

Tapasyananda, Swami. *Bhakti Schools of Vedanta ; Lives and Philosophies of Ramanuja, Nimbarka, Madhava, Vallabha and Caitanya*. Vedanta Press, n.d.

Tolle, Eckhart. *A New Earth: Awakening to Your Life's Purpose*. Plume, 2006.

Traherne, Thomas. *Centuries of Meditations*. Christian Classics Ethereal Library, 2009.

Tyagananda, Swami. "Katha Upanishad." Boston: Vedanta Society of Boston, 9 February 2007.

Underhill, Evelyn. *The Ways of the Spirit*. Ed. Grace Aldophsen Brame. The Crossroad Publishing Company, 1993.

Vivekananda, Swami. *Jnana Yoga*. Ramakrishna-Vivekananda Center, 1982.

—. *Karma Yoga*. Ramakrishna-Vivekananda Center, 1982.

—. *Raja Yoga*. Ramakrishna-Vivekananda Center, 1982.

Voragine, Jacobus de. *The Golden Legend: Lives of the Saints*. Vol. 4. Christian Classics Ethereal Library, 1914.

Walker, Pete. *Complex PTSD: From Surviving to Thriving: A Guide and Map for Recovering from Childhood Trauma*. CreateSpace Independent Publishing Platform, 2013.

Wesley, Charles. "A Thought on Judgment." In Nutter, Charles Sumner and Fisk, Wilbur. *An Annotated Edition of the Methodist Hymnal*, 1911.

White, E. B. *Charlotte's Web*. Trophy Newbury, 2012.

Wikipedia. *Perennial Philosophy*. 6 June 2015.
<http://en.wikipedia.org/wiki/Perennial_philosophy>

Williamson, Marianne. *A Return to Love*. HarperOne, 2012.

Wu, John C.H. *The Golden Age of Zen: Zen Masters of the T'ang Dynasty*. World Wisdom, 2003.

About the Author

Photo by Allison Ballantine

Rev. Dr. Scott Robinson has worked as a college music instructor, a composer, an actor-musician, and a journalist. An ordained Interfaith Minister, he currently divides his time between hospice chaplaincy, writing, leading workshops and retreats, and performing his original music with his band Mandala. You can learn more about his work at www.opentothedivine.com.